45

D1434025

740006497121

GADGETS, GAMES, ROBOTS, AND THE DIGITAL WORLD

London, New York,
Melbourne, Munich, and Delhi

Senior editor Francesca Baines
Senior art editor Smiljka Surla

Editors Clare Hibbert, James Mitchem
Art editors Angela Ball, Dave Ball, Daniela Boraschi

Managing editor Linda Esposito
Managing art editor Jim Green

Category Publisher Laura Buller

HEREFORDSHIRE
LIBRARIES

712	
Bertrams	09/09/2013
J004.16	£14.99
HS	

…fomen, Charis Tsevis

…Graef

…er
…o Tahata
…a M Tampakopoulos Turner

First published in Great Britain in 2011 by
Dorling Kindersley Limited,
80 Strand, London, WC2R 0RL

Copyright © 2011 Dorling Kindersley Limited
A Penguin Company

2 4 6 8 10 9 7 5 3 1
001 –179073 – 05/11

All rights reserved. No part of this publication may be reproduced,
stored in a retrieval system, or transmitted in any form or by any means,
electronic, mechanical, photocopying, recording, or otherwise, without
the prior written permission of the copyright owner.

A CIP catalogue record for this book
is available from the British Library

ISBN: 978-1-40536-785-1

Hi-res workflow proofed by MDP, UK
Printed and bound by Toppan, China

Discover more at
www.dk.com

GADGETS, GAMES, ROBOTS, AND THE DIGITAL WORLD

Written by **Clive Gifford**
Consultant **Dr Mike Goldsmith**

Contents

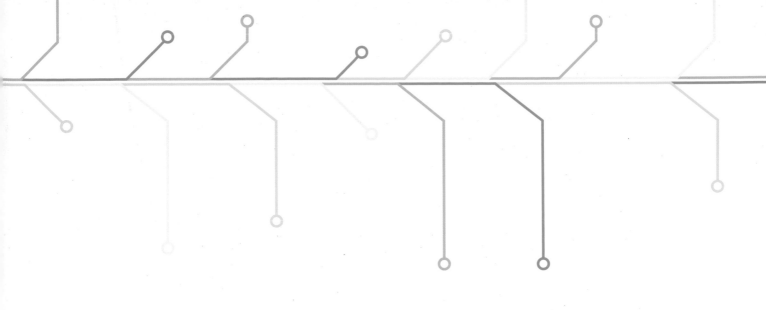

Calculators and **computers**

"I wish to God these calculations had been executed by steam," Charles Babbage exclaimed, poring over a mistake-filled volume of mathematical tables. The year was 1821, when such books were the only help for number-crunchers. So Babbage set out to mechanize how these tables were produced, and along the way became the first computing pioneer.

Did you know?

For more than 2,000 years, the abacus was the only common and reliable means of making calculations using a machine.

Charles Babbage

Having taught himself algebra as a child, English inventor Charles Babbage (1791–1871) was a highly regarded mathematician by his twenties. In 1828, he was awarded the Lucasian Chair of Mathematics at Cambridge, a distinguished position held earlier by Sir Isaac Newton. Babbage would later invent lighthouse signalling devices and cowcatchers for steam trains. He also became a master code maker and breaker and an expert economist.

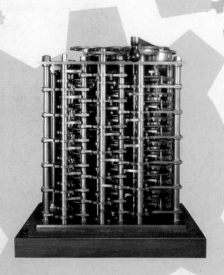

The Difference Engine

In 1823, the British government gave Babbage the go-ahead to start work on a machine for calculating mathematical tables. He designed two giant calculators, called Difference Engines, the first of which (left) required 25,000 iron and brass parts! With no electricity, both machines were designed to be powered by hand.

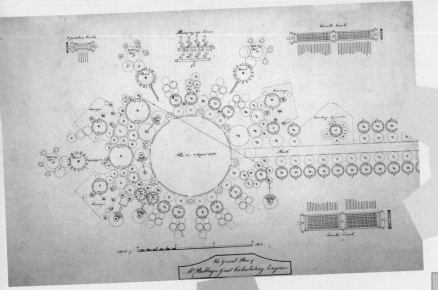

Birth of the computer

In the 1830s, Babbage abandoned his first Difference Engine to devote his attention to an even more ambitious plan, as shown in his complex design from 1840 (left). His steam-driven, mechanical Analytical Engine was to be a general purpose "computer", capable of all sorts of calculations, and directed by programmed instructions. Conceived decades before the invention of electronics, it was utterly revolutionary and uncannily like the design of modern computers.

↗ How it worked

The Analytical Engine was never actually made. If it had been, it would have been programmable using punched cards.

◉ The "mill" was the central processor where arithmetic was performed. It retrieved and executed instructions and data from the "store" just like a modern computer.

◉ The "store" was the engine's expandable memory, capable of holding results and data during calculations.

◉ Results could be sent to the engine's own printer and graph plotter or onto punched cards.

> "Babbage's reputation has been vindicated, both as a visionary of the computer age and, more specifically, as an engineer of the most extraordinary calibre."
>
> Doron Swade, curator of the Science Museum, London, UK

Failure

Babbage's engines were not completed in his lifetime. The sheer ambition of his designs, his perfectionism, disputes over costs, a struggle for funds, and problems engineering the highly accurate parts required (above), were the main reasons for this failure. "Another age must be the judge," Babbage admitted.

Did you know?

Almost 200 years after Babbage was born, the Science Museum in London, UK, built his second Difference Engine using the original blueprints. It has more than 4,000 parts, and what's more, it works!

The countess

Daughter of the poet Lord Byron, English mathematician Augusta Ada King, Countess of Lovelace, first met Babbage in 1833. Translating an article about his work in 1842–3, her notes included algorithms (instructions for solving mathematical problems) that effectively make her one of the first programmers. A 1979 computer language was named Ada in her honour.

The great brain

It is 1947, and the world's fastest general purpose electronic computer is at work, churning through top-secret calculations for the American hydrogen bomb programme. Dubbed the "great brain" by the press, the Electronic Numerical Integrator and Computer (ENIAC) weighed in at 27,000 kg (60,000 lb) and consumed as much power as 15,000 iPads. At the machine's heart lay vacuum tubes – electrical components able to amplify electrical signals or act as switches (that break or make electrical circuits). A radio of the time might contain 10 vacuum tubes, but this beast boasted 17,468 of them.

Building ENIAC

J Presper Eckert (right) was just out of his teens when he and Dr John Mauchly began work on ENIAC. Completed in 1945, ENIAC ran for a decade. Eckert and Mauchly also formed their own company to produce UNIVAC I, the first computer to go on sale to the public in the USA.

Did you know?

To work out which type of wire to use to build ENIAC, J Presper Eckert starved lab rats for a few days. Then he gave them samples of different types of cable to determine which they gnawed through the least.

Massive machine

No wonder ENIAC took 3 years to build. It was 30 m (98 ft) long, more than 3 m (10 ft) high, and 1 m (3 ft) deep. Its 40 front panels, which were arranged in a U-shape, required hundreds of thousands of hand-soldered joints.

Women's work

Six female mathematicians programmed ENIAC. Their job title was "Computer". Although ENIAC worked quickly, changing its program could be tedious because its panels had to be rewired, a process that could take up to 2 days.

Shrunk on silicon

From ENIAC onwards, computers advanced rapidly and their speed accelerated as their components shrank in size. In 1997, students at the University of Pennsylvania, USA, recreated ENIAC on just one silicon chip (left). While ENIAC could perform 5,000 operations per second, an Intel Core Duo chip today can manage 21.6 billion.

"We're flooding people with information. We need to feed it through a processor. A human must turn information into intelligence or knowledge. We've tended to forget that no computer will ever ask a new question."

Grace Hopper

A gifted mathematician, Grace Hopper (1906–92) joined the US Navy during World War II. There, she became the first woman to program the Harvard Mark I, a pioneering computer based at Harvard University, USA. Then, in 1949, Hopper joined the Eckert-Mauchly Corporation and worked on the first commercial computer, UNIVAC I. Her greatest contributions, though, came in the 1950s. She developed the first compilers, progams that made programming far easier, and also worked on the first high-level computer language for business, the Common Business-Oriented Language (COBOL), still in use today.

Did you know?

Hopper popularized the terms "bug" and "debugging" (to remove errors in computer code) after an incident when a moth was trapped inside part of a computer at Harvard University, USA.

1/1

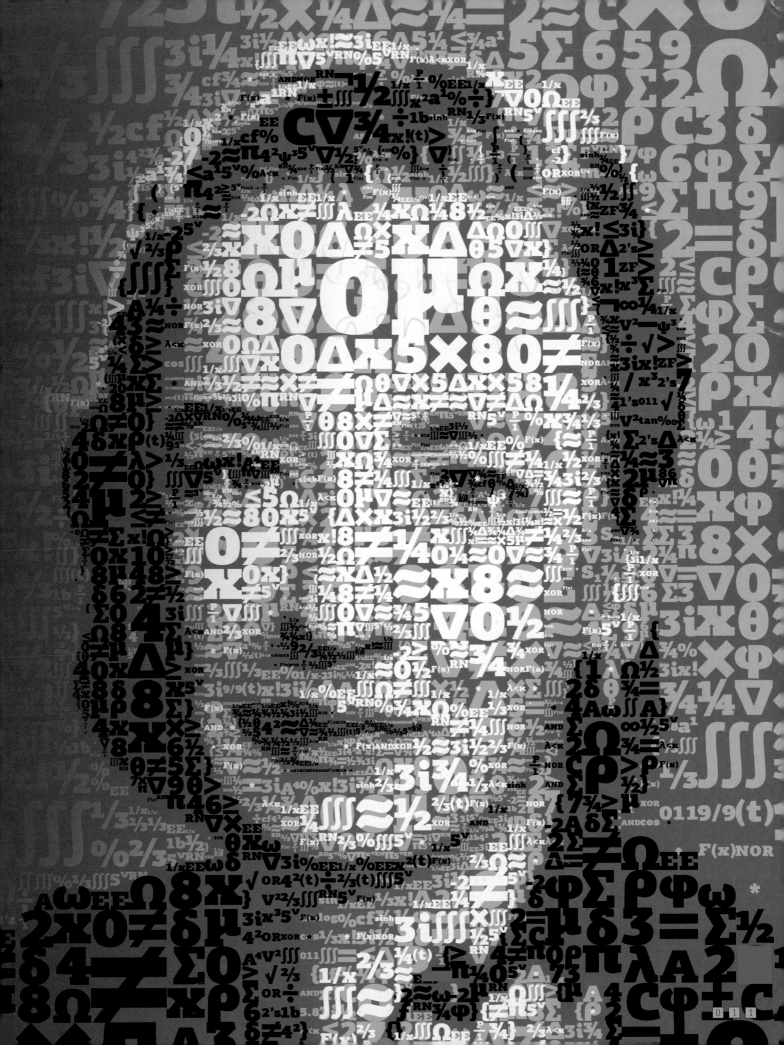

Evolution of the computer

Computers took a long time coming. They developed out of centuries of attempts at getting machines to help perform complex calculations. A burst of innovation before, during, and after World War II led to the arrivals of the jet engine, the atomic bomb, and the first practical computers. In the decades since then, computers have advanced at a spectacular rate.

↑ 1642
Blaise Pascal creates the Pascaline, one of the first mechanical adding machines.

↑ 3000 BCE
The abacus counting device is invented in Babylonia.

↓ 1822
Charles Babbage begins work on his Difference Engine.

1936
Alan Turing develops the concept of a theoretical computing machine.

↑ 1939–45
In the US, UK, and Germany, mechanical and electric calculators and computing-styled machines, such as the Harvard Mark I (see part of it above), are developed. They crack codes, calculate firing tables for artillery, and help in other ways with the war effort.

1938
In Berlin, Germany, Konrad Zuse completes the first binary programmable mechanical computer, the Z1. His Z3, the first true electronic computer, follows in 1941.

1946
J Presper Eckert and John Mauchly complete the Electronic Numerical Integrator and Computer (ENIAC). It is one of the first digital computers.

1946
John von Neumann proposes that a program can be stored in a computer the same way data is. His proposal of "von Neumann architecture" for computers becomes the basis for modern machines.

↓ 1952
Tom Cranston and Fred Longstaff invent the trackball input device, using a bowling ball at the centre of their apparatus.

1952
Grace Hopper and her team complete the first compiler, a program that allows a computer operator to use words instead of numbers.

1623
Wilhelm Schickard invents the mechanical calculator.

↓ 1666
Samuel Morland produces a pocket-sized mechanical calculator capable of addition and subtraction.

1854
The English philosopher George Boole develops Boolean logic and algebra, using binary numbers (ones and zeroes) – the basis of modern computer logic.

↓ 1890
This year's US Census is completed in record time thanks to Herman Hollerith's invention of an automated tabulating machine, using punched cards as storage. Hollerith's company merges with others in 1911 to form IBM.

↑ 1939
Hewlett-Packard is founded in a garage in Palo Alto, California, USA. Eight models of its first product, a sound generator, are bought by Walt Disney for its 1940 animation, *Fantasia*.

1948
The first computer to store its programs and data in electronic memory, the Manchester Baby, begins operation. The following year, it is upgraded with magnetic-drum storage to become the Manchester Mark I.

↓ 1956
The first hard disk drive, the IBM Model 350 Disk File, goes on sale with the IBM 305 RAMAC computer. It weighs around a tonne and holds up to 5 MB of data. Users can rent 1 MB of storage on the device for £80 (US$130) a month

A life in computing

As a 15-year-old in 1982, Rich Skrenta created Elk Cloner, one of the first computer viruses. It was transmitted on floppy disks between early Apple computers. Skrenta went on to work for Commodore, Sun Microsystems, and AOL. He helped form the Open Directory Project (a collection of World Wide Web links) and, in 2010, launched a major new search engine, Blekko.

"This is only a foretaste of what is to come, and only the shadow of what is going to be… I do not see why [computers] should not enter any of the fields normally covered by the human intellect."

Alan Turing, 1949. Turing (1912–1954) was an English mathematician and cryptanalyst (code breaker), and one of the founders of modern computer science.

↓ 1964
John Kemeny and Thomas Kurtz develop the BASIC (Beginner's All-purpose Symbolic Instruction Code) programming language, which will drive the first boom of home computers in the 1970s and '80s.

← 1971
The Intel 4004 microprocessor chip, designed by Ted Hoff, is the first complete central processing unit (CPU).

↑ 1982
The Commodore C64 home computer is released. It goes on to sell 22 million units, far more than any other single model of personal computer.

↓ 1968
Douglas Engelbart showcases the mouse (first built in 1963), hypertext, and onscreen videoconferencing in a multimedia demonstration.

↑ 1993
Intel releases the first Pentium microprocessor chip.

1961
Jack Kilby and Robert Noyce develop the silicon chip, laying many integrated circuits on a single wafer of silicon.

↓ 1996
The Universal Serial Bus (USB) 1.0 standard is established, allowing different makes of peripherals to communicate with computers. The faster USB 2.0 is introduced 4 years later.

↑ 1977
Radio Shack unveils its fully assembled microcomputer, the TRS-80 Model I, with keyboard, monitor, and cassette unit.

1978
VisiCalc, the first automatic recalculating spreadsheet software for personal computers, is released.

↑ 1984
Apple advertise their Macintosh computer, the first big-selling computer with a graphic user interface and a mouse.

1963
ASCII, the American Standard Code for Information Interchange, is announced. It allows computers from different manufacturers to exchange data.

1969
Gary Starkweather, a researcher at Xerox, invents the laser printer. IBM will sell the first laser printer, the 3800, from 1975 onwards.

↓ 1981
IBM launches its Personal Computer (PC). It sells more than three million units and its operating system, Microsoft MS-DOS, becomes the standard for business programs.

1985
Aldus announces its PageMaker program for use on Macintosh computers, launching an interest in desktop publishing.

2001
Microsoft releases its Windows XP operating system. As of 2010, it powers more PCs than any other operating system.

↓ 2007
The first netbook, the Asus Eee PC 701, goes on sale in October. More than 300,000 are sold before the end of the year.

↓ 1965
Digital Equipment Corp (DEC) puts on sale the first commercially successful minicomputer, the PDP-8.

1975
Bill Gates and Paul Allen found Microsoft.

1991
A Finnish college student, Linus Torvalds, begins building Linux, a free operating system for PCs. It goes on to become the third most popular operating system family, after Windows and Mac. Versions of Linux are found everywhere, from smartphones and netbooks to supercomputers.

1976
Steve Jobs, Steve Wozniak, and Ronald Wayne found Apple Computer, a company to sell their Apple I computer.

A vision of
the future

Did you know?
During World War II, the young Engelbart worked as a radar technician for the US Navy. His knowledge of how radar information was displayed onscreen inspired his 1951 vision of how hypertext might work.

Every time you use a mouse to click on a link to a new web page, you have American electrical engineer Douglas Engelbart to thank. Engelbart was an early computer pioneer. As far back as 1951, he imagined screens with information flowing between them, and people navigating the screens to learn, form, and organize their ideas. Sounds familiar? He could be describing the Internet and hypertext – text with active links to other pages.

Douglas Engelbart

Born in 1925, Engelbart studied electrical engineering. In 1957 he joined the Stanford Research Institute (SRI), California, where he was later given his own research lab. There, his team developed the revolutionary oNLine System (NLS). This allowed up to 16 workstations to operate together, running programs with multiple windows between which text and objects could move.

New controls
In the early 1950s, very few computers existed, and they were controlled by experts and engineers using punched cards or rewiring circuits. Engelbart's vision demanded faster, simpler, more natural ways of working. His team developed cursors that could be dragged around the screen. They also experimented with chorded keysets (keyboards), where pressing down different combinations of five piano-like keys created commands.

First mouse

In 1963, Engelbart and a colleague, Bill English, invented the first computer mouse. The name came from the tail-like cable that ran from the back of the wooden box. Known more formally as an "X–Y position indicator for a display system", the device had a single click switch and two metal wheels positioned at 90 degrees to each other that kept track of up-and-down and side-to-side movement. Computer mice only became popular 20 years later.

↗

The mother of all demos

San Francisco, 1968

At a conference in 1968, Engelbart gave a demonstration to 1,000 computer experts that would make them think about computers in a totally new way. In what became known as the "mother of all demos", his presentation included:

❍ Documents being edited in multiple windows by different people on different computers.

❍ The computer mouse, wordprocessing, instant messaging, and hypertext between documents, files, and programs.

❍ Real-time videoconferencing between Engelbart and staff at his laboratory approximately 60 km (37 miles) away (above).

"Computer technology is going to blossom so spectacularly, and hit our society so hard, that I am both thrilled and frightened... Imagine what it might be like to have information-handling 'horsepower' available for your personal use."
Douglas Engelbart, 1961

Inspirational teacher

Engelbart's work has won more than 30 awards, including the £300,000 (US$500,000) Lemelson–MIT Prize (1997) and the US National Medal of Technology (2000), which was presented by President Clinton. Over his career Engelbart influenced many other computing pioneers, including those he collaborated with on early Internet projects. Some of Engelbart's staff went on to the Xerox PARC research facility, where they developed the first graphical user interfaces, allowing users to interact with systems by clicking on icons on a screen rather than typing in commands.

ZX81 →

In 1981, British inventor Clive Sinclair released the ZX81. It had a mere 1 KB of memory, a barely-usable keyboard, and it had to be hooked up to a television to display its black-and-white text and rudimentary graphics, but it was a revelation. The ZX81's launch price was just £69.99 in the UK and US$99.99 in the USA. Computers had never been so affordable before.

Commodore 64 →

By 1982, the home computer market was starting to mature. One of the most popular computers of the time was the Commodore 64. The C64 had a proper keyboard, a then enormous 64 KB of internal memory, a built-in sound synthesizer, and more advanced graphics than any of its rivals.

← Spectrum

Sinclair's successor to the ZX81, the Spectrum, released in 1982, had a moving, rubber-key keyboard, 16 KB or 48 KB of memory, and colour graphics. It was still primitive, but a growing band of computer enthusiasts wrote all sorts of software for it, including games, such as *Horace Goes Skiing* and *Chuckie Egg*, and astronomy and accounting packages.

Early home computing

In the mid-1970s only a handful of electronics enthusiasts owned computers, which they had built from kits. Then, from the late 1970s, affordable microcomputers gave millions of people their first direct taste of computing. The boom spawned numerous cottage industries in computer books, magazines, software, and games.

TRS-80 →

Priced at £375 (US$600), including a black-and-white monitor, the TRS-80 went on sale in 3,000 Radio Shack and Tandy stores from December 1977. More than 400,000 machines were sold, as well as business software, such as *Payroll* and *Statistical Analysis*, and of course, games. A colour version of the computer, the TRS-80 CoCo, followed 3 years later.

← BASIC

Computer owners of the 1970s and early '80s often wrote their own programs using an instruction language known as BASIC. It had easy-to-learn commands, such as IF-THEN decision statements and GOTO to navigate to a numbered line of program code. Many of today's tech experts learned their trade on this surprisingly flexible computer language.

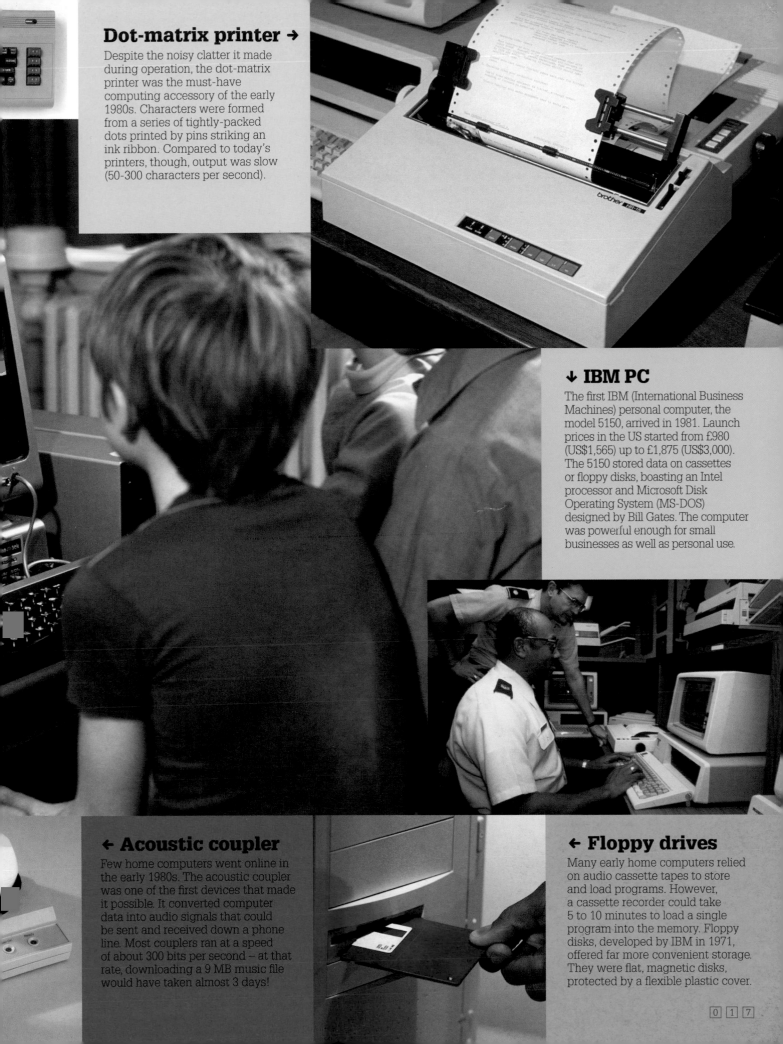

Dot-matrix printer →

Despite the noisy clatter it made during operation, the dot-matrix printer was the must-have computing accessory of the early 1980s. Characters were formed from a series of tightly-packed dots printed by pins striking an ink ribbon. Compared to today's printers, though, output was slow (50-300 characters per second).

↓ IBM PC

The first IBM (International Business Machines) personal computer, the model 5150, arrived in 1981. Launch prices in the US started from £980 (US$1,565) up to £1,875 (US$3,000). The 5150 stored data on cassettes or floppy disks, boasting an Intel processor and Microsoft Disk Operating System (MS-DOS) designed by Bill Gates. The computer was powerful enough for small businesses as well as personal use.

← Acoustic coupler

Few home computers went online in the early 1980s. The acoustic coupler was one of the first devices that made it possible. It converted computer data into audio signals that could be sent and received down a phone line. Most couplers ran at a speed of about 300 bits per second – at that rate, downloading a 9 MB music file would have taken almost 3 days!

← Floppy drives

Many early home computers relied on audio cassette tapes to store and load programs. However, a cassette recorder could take 5 to 10 minutes to load a single program into the memory. Floppy disks, developed by IBM in 1971, offered far more convenient storage. They were flat, magnetic disks, protected by a flexible plastic cover.

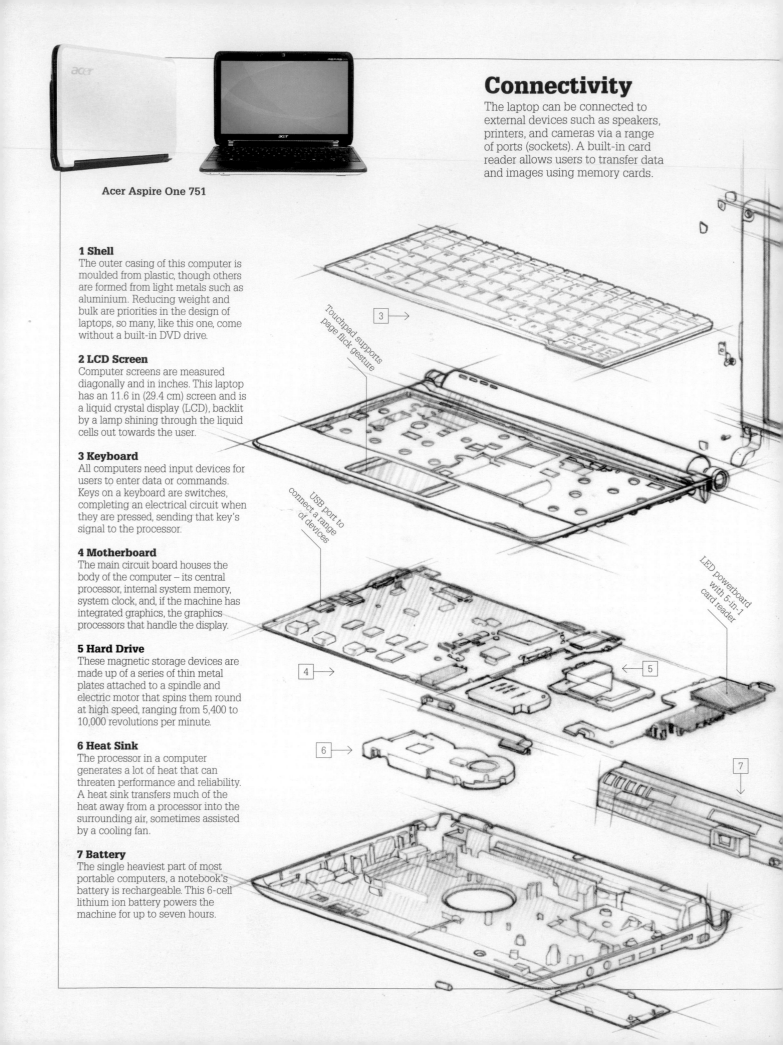

Acer Aspire One 751

Connectivity

The laptop can be connected to external devices such as speakers, printers, and cameras via a range of ports (sockets). A built-in card reader allows users to transfer data and images using memory cards.

1 Shell
The outer casing of this computer is moulded from plastic, though others are formed from light metals such as aluminium. Reducing weight and bulk are priorities in the design of laptops, so many, like this one, come without a built-in DVD drive.

2 LCD Screen
Computer screens are measured diagonally and in inches. This laptop has an 11.6 in (29.4 cm) screen and is a liquid crystal display (LCD), backlit by a lamp shining through the liquid cells out towards the user.

3 Keyboard
All computers need input devices for users to enter data or commands. Keys on a keyboard are switches, completing an electrical circuit when they are pressed, sending that key's signal to the processor.

4 Motherboard
The main circuit board houses the body of the computer – its central processor, internal system memory, system clock, and, if the machine has integrated graphics, the graphics processors that handle the display.

5 Hard Drive
These magnetic storage devices are made up of a series of thin metal plates attached to a spindle and electric motor that spins them round at high speed, ranging from 5,400 to 10,000 revolutions per minute.

6 Heat Sink
The processor in a computer generates a lot of heat that can threaten performance and reliability. A heat sink transfers much of the heat away from a processor into the surrounding air, sometimes assisted by a cooling fan.

7 Battery
The single heaviest part of most portable computers, a notebook's battery is rechargeable. This 6-cell lithium ion battery powers the machine for up to seven hours.

Touchpad supports page flick gesture

USB port to connect a range of devices

LED powerboard with 5-in-1 card reader

3

4

5

6

7

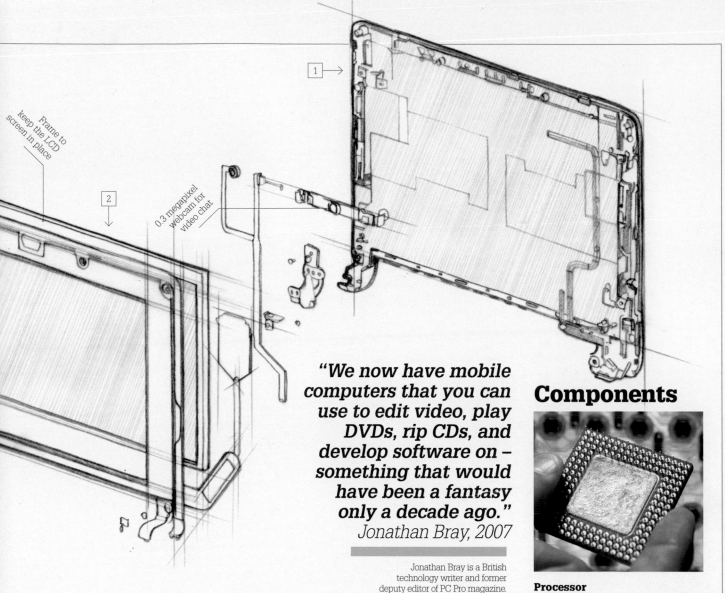

Frame to keep the LCD screen in place

1

2

0.3 megapixel webcam for video chat

"We now have mobile computers that you can use to edit video, play DVDs, rip CDs, and develop software on – something that would have been a fantasy only a decade ago."
Jonathan Bray, 2007

Jonathan Bray is a British technology writer and former deputy editor of PC Pro magazine.

Laptop

Laptops and their smaller, lighter, and usually less powerful cousins, netbooks, allow people to keep in touch, work, learn, or play when on the move. They take up little space, yet the most powerful can compete in performance with many far bulkier desktop machines. Early portable computers with only a fraction of the capability of a modern machine often weighed more than 10 kg (22 lb). The Acer Aspire One 751 featured here weighs a mere 1.25 kg (2.7 lb).

Components

Processor
A CPU (central processing unit) is the computer's brains. It is capable of performing the machine's calculations at rates measured in the millions per second. The Atom Z520 processor used in the Aspire One is common in many small, lightweight netbooks.

RAM
Random access memory (RAM) is a circuit that holds data and gives the computer's processor, and any running programs, their own area in which to perform and store processes and data.

→ Networks

A computer network involves two or more computers, known as nodes, linked so that they can communicate electronically with each other. Networks can be wired, with cables physically connecting the computers, or wireless, with radio waves or satellite signals linking them. Once connected, computers can exchange data, including sound and image files.

ISPs

In return for a monthly or annual fee, an Internet Service Provider (ISP) provides millions of businesses and homes with Internet access via telephone, cable, or satellite links. The first public ISP was TheWorld, which opened in 1989 in Brookline, Massachusetts, USA.

Home networks

A typical home computer network might consist of two or three PCs that share a printer, scanner, or a large hard drive for backup storage. Each device has its own network address so that other devices can identify and communicate with it using rules called protocols.

LANs and WANs

A typical office has a number of machines networked over a small area. The above office LAN (Local Area Network) may use a router to connect to other nearby LANs. A number of LANs may connect to form a WAN (Wide Area Network), which operates over great distances.

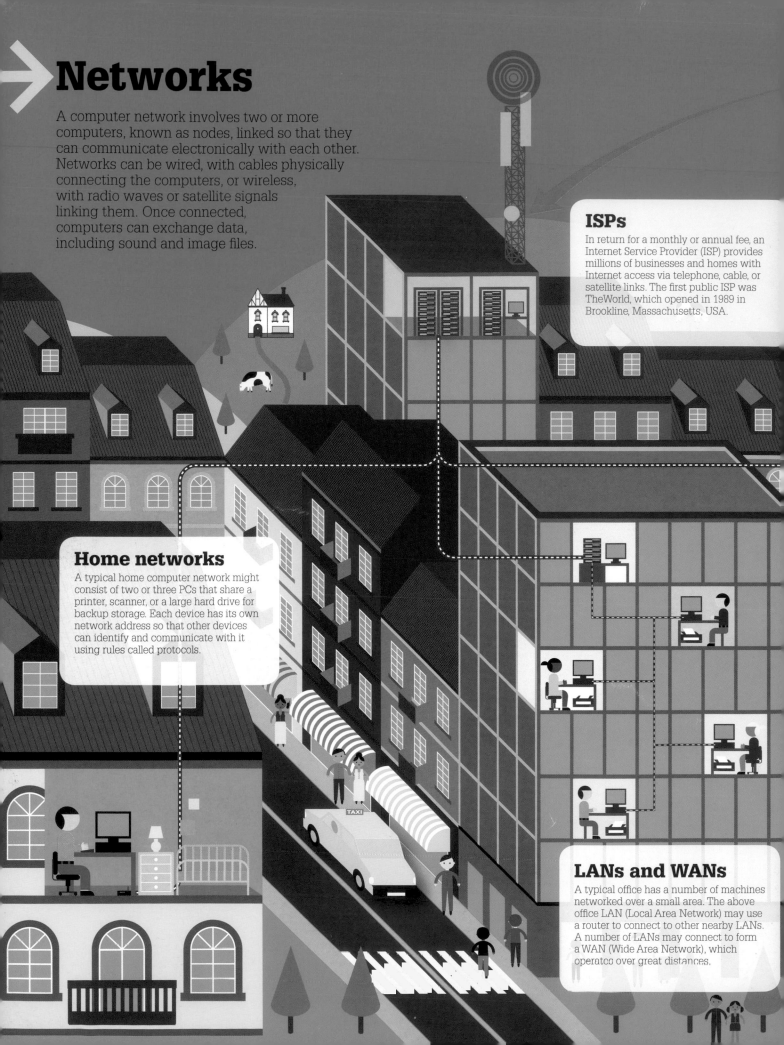

Satellites

Satellites orbiting Earth can relay data to and from computers to enable access to the Internet. This is particularly valuable in rural communities with no access to cable networks. All users need is a dish placed in unobstructed view of the skyline, in order to access the Internet directly.

Did you know?

The Virtual Internet Cafe opened in 2008. Based online, it allows users to control its computers remotely so that they can surf the Internet without exposing their own PCs to malware.

Around the world

The Internet is the biggest WAN of all. It consists of vast numbers of networks – from small LANs to huge academic or governmental networks – all linked together using common protocols. Many ISPs' networks interconnect at locations called access points or Internet exchanges.

Did you know?

The first Internet "café in a box" was installed in Zambia by the Computer Aid charity in 2010. A shipping container was fitted with 11 computers powered by solar panels on the container's roof.

High School

Cybercafés

The first Internet café opened in San Francisco in 1991. For a purchase of food or drink or a small fee, cybercafés offer use of a computer connected to the Internet or a Wi-Fi hotspot for your own PC. In countries with low computer ownership, most people access the Net in cafés.

Café

Server network

The computers in this school network are linked to a central computer, called a server, which controls some tasks, like printing, on behalf of the other computers called clients. This is a client-server network. An alternative is a peer-to-peer network where all the computers perform the same range of tasks.

Inventing the
World Wide Web

On 25 December 1990, Tim Berners-Lee set a new task for a computer at the European Organization for Nuclear Research (CERN) laboratory in Switzerland. The computer was a prototype web server. It hosted the world's first web page, which described the World Wide Web and showed others how to start their own websites. Before this event, the Internet was the mostly text-based domain of scientists and other academics.

> ORGANISATION EUROPÉENNE POUR LA RECHERCHE
> **CERN** EUROPEAN ORGANIZATION FOR NUCLEAR
> 1211 GENÈVE 23 (SUISSE)
>
> This machine is a server
> DO NOT POWE
> ... DOWN!!

ENQUIRE

In 1980, Berners-Lee wrote a program called ENQUIRE for use inside CERN to track the connections between different people and projects using hyperlinks (see pages 16–17). Ten years later, he would use similar principles to create a web of hyperlinked documents on the Internet – the World Wide Web. This was first hosted on a single computer on which Berners-Lee scrawled on the back, "This machine is a server. Do not power it down."

Did you know?

In a 2009 interview in *The Times* newspaper, Berners-Lee admitted that the "//" (two forward slashes) in web addresses had not really been necessary. "There you go – it seemed like a good idea at the time," he joked.

Following footsteps

Tim Berners-Lee was born in England in 1955. His parents, Conway and Mary Berners-Lee, had met three years earlier at Ferranti, where they both worked as mathematicians on the Mark 1 computer. Tim studied physics at Oxford, where he built his own first computer from some logic gates, an M6800 processor, and old television parts. Berners-Lee followed his parents' footsteps and began working as a software consultant at CERN in 1980.

Options Navigate Hotlist Annotate

Document Title: I NCSA Mosaic Home Page‖

Document URL: http://www.ncsa.uiuc.edu/SDG/Software/Mosaic/NCSAMosaicHome.html

N C S A

MOSAIC
X Window System • Microsoft Windows • Macintosh

Welcome to NCSA Mosaic, an Internet information browser and World Wide Web client. NCSA
Mosaic was developed at the National Center for Supercomputing Applications at the
University of Illinois in --> Urbana-Champaign. NCSA Mosaic software is copyrighted by
The Board of Trustees of the University of Illinois (UI), and ownership remains with the
UI.

Jan '97

The Software Development Group at NCSA has worked on NCSA Mosaic for nearly four years
and we've learned a lot in the process. We are honored that we were able to help bring
this technology to the masses and appreciated all the support and feedback we have
received in return. However, the time has come for us to concentrate our limited
resources in other areas of interest and development on Mosaic is complete.

All information about the Mosaic project is available from the homepages.

NCSA Mosaic Platforms:

● NCSA Mosaic for the X Window System
♦ NCSA Mosaic for the Apple Macintosh
  NCSA Mosaic for Microsoft Windows

W3C

In 1994, Berners-Lee moved to head the World Wide Web Consortium (W3C), a group devoted to improving the Web. He campaigned hard to keep it open and free. Nearly 20 years on, he is still a director of the W3C, as well as a respected advisor and researcher for governments and academic bodies.

Browsers

One boost to the early World Wide Web was the development of new, more user- and graphics-friendly browser programs (see panel, right). Marc Andreessen and colleagues at the University of Illinois, USA, developed the Mosaic browser, which became available in 1993. Mosaic helped to popularize browsing, and the number of websites started to mushroom.

> "The Web as I envisaged it, we have not seen it yet. The future is still so much bigger than the past."
>
> *Tim Berners-Lee, 2009*

↗ The invention of the Web

In the late 1980s, Berners-Lee proposed building a hyperlink-based information system for use over the Internet. Working with a Belgian computer engineer, Robert Cailliau (above left, displaying the first server computer in the museum at CERN) and others, Berners-Lee had to assemble a number of different elements to get the World Wide Web up and running:

⊙ HTML Berners-Lee needed a standard language to create hypertext documents that could be retrieved and viewed on different computers all over the world. The answer was hypertext markup language (HTML), which uses tags as instructions, allowing pages to display different text sizes and colours, pictures, and other files.

⊙ HTTP The team developed the hypertext transfer protocol (HTTP), a system that allowed computers to communicate hypertext documents over the Internet.

⊙ Browser Berners-Lee and his colleagues wrote the first web browser – a program that could find, retrieve, and view hypertext documents. Initially called "WorldWideWeb", it was renamed "Nexus" to avoid confusion with the Web itself.

⊙ Web server The software that stores web pages on a computer and makes them available to others – a server – had to be created. In 1990, Berners-Lee set up the first web server at CERN with the address "http://info.cern.ch".

Web explosion

The World Wide Web became available over the Internet in August 1991, with just one server hosting a single website. Ten years later, there were 36 million websites and by 2011, more than 250 million. This boom was helped early on by CERN's decision to make the World Wide Web free for use by everyone.

Undersea cables

In a secret location, buried 2 m (6 ft) beneath the sands of a beach – possibly this beach – in Cornwall, on the western tip of Britain, lies a £250 million (US$ 400 million) cable not much thicker than a garden hose. This high-capacity Internet cable links New York and London, the busiest hubs in the world. In fact, around 90 per cent of global Internet traffic is carried by a vast cable network that snakes over land and sea, with more than 800,000 km (500,000 miles) of cabling found underwater.

Top secret
The location of the British beach the cable passes under is a secret. The cabling station, just set back from the beach, does not appear on any map.

High speed
It takes a fraction of a second for data to travel the 12,200-km (7,600-mile) return trip from the UK to the USA. About every 49 km (30 miles) or so, the signals get a boost from amplifier devices called repeaters. Each repeater costs around £1 million (US$1.5 million).

Did you know?
When the first transatlantic fibre-optic cables were laid in the 1980s, they attracted sharks, resulting in severed cables and electrocuted sharks. The cables were quickly enclosed in a protective casing.

Running repairs

The robot below is being lowered into the sea where it will crawl the seabed repairing damaged cables. In 2009, millions of Internet users in India saw their connections wiped out after a ship's anchor cut a cable. If a cable breaks, data is usually re-routed until repairs are completed.

Fibre optics

Bundled inside the main transatlantic cable, the OALC-4 SPDA, are eight fibre-optic cables, each the width of a single human hair and with enough bandwidth for 20 million people. In the USA the cables emerge from beneath the Atlantic Ocean at a vast server centre that channels the data to around 150 countries.

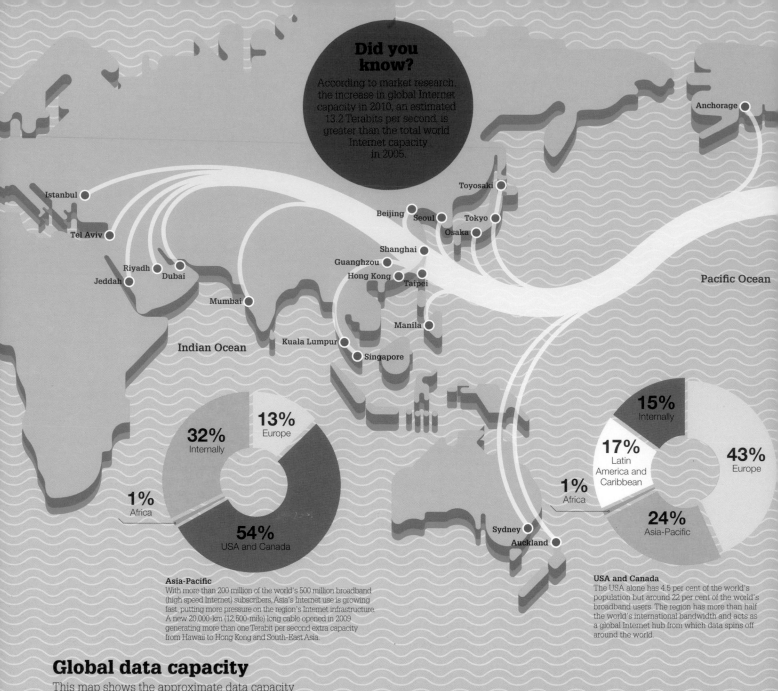

Did you know?

According to market research, the increase in global Internet capacity in 2010, an estimated 13.2 Terabits per second, is greater than the total world Internet capacity in 2005.

Anchorage

Istanbul

Tel Aviv

Riyadh — Dubai

Jeddah

Mumbai

Indian Ocean

Toyosaki

Beijing — Seoul — Tokyo

Osaka

Shanghai

Guanghzou

Hong Kong — Taipei

Manila

Kuala Lumpur

Singapore

Pacific Ocean

Asia-Pacific

- 13% Europe
- 32% Internally
- 54% USA and Canada
- 1% Africa

With more than 200 million of the world's 500 million broadband (high speed Internet) subscribers, Asia's Internet use is growing fast, putting more pressure on the region's Internet infrastructure. A new 20,000-km (12,500-mile) long cable opened in 2009 generating more than one Terabit per second extra capacity from Hawaii to Hong Kong and South-East Asia.

USA and Canada

- 15% Internally
- 17% Latin America and Caribbean
- 43% Europe
- 24% Asia-Pacific
- 1% Africa

The USA alone has 4.5 per cent of the world's population but around 22 per cent of the world's broadband users. The region has more than half the world's international bandwidth and acts as a global Internet hub from which data spins off around the world.

Sydney

Auckland

Global data capacity

This map shows the approximate data capacity (bandwidth) between many of the world's busiest cities, major Internet hubs like London, New York, and Shanghai. The circular charts detail what percentage of a region's bandwidth is connected to other regions.

Internet traffic

When you click on a link to visit a website, your request and the web page you eventually see have travelled as data, a tiny part of the vast flow of data over worldwide Internet networks. The measure of how much data can be sent over a network at once is called the bandwidth of the connection. As more and more people get connected, Internet traffic continues to rise. In 2009 alone it increased by 74 per cent, and then by a further 62 per cent in 2010. The Internet's infrastructure must continue to grow to cope with this ever increasing demand.

Did you know?

According to a 2010 Internet report, at peak time, 43 per cent of Internet traffic in North America is taken up by real-time entertainment such as streaming videos, audio, and games.

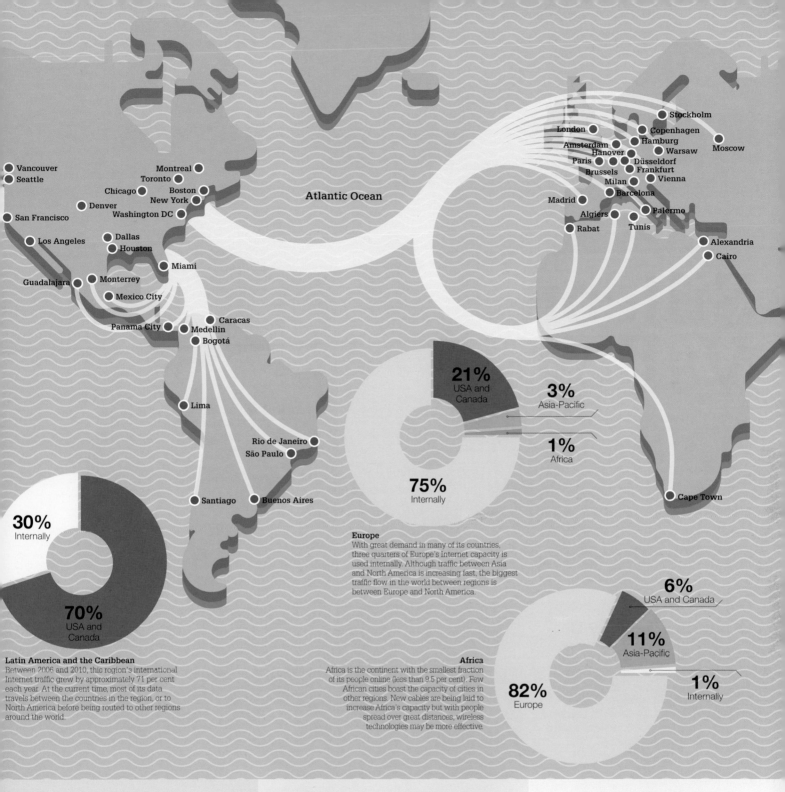

Vancouver
Seattle
Montreal
Toronto
Chicago
Denver
Boston
New York
Washington DC
San Francisco
Los Angeles
Dallas
Houston
Miami
Guadalajara
Monterrey
Mexico City
Panama City
Caracas
Medellín
Bogotá
Lima
Rio de Janeiro
São Paulo
Santiago
Buenos Aires

London
Amsterdam
Hanover
Paris
Brussels
Madrid
Algiers
Rabat
Stockholm
Copenhagen
Hamburg
Warsaw
Moscow
Düsseldorf
Frankfurt
Vienna
Milan
Barcelona
Palermo
Tunis
Alexandria
Cairo
Cape Town

Atlantic Ocean

21%
USA and Canada

3%
Asia-Pacific

1%
Africa

75%
Internally

Europe
With great demand in many of its countries, three quarters of Europe's Internet capacity is used internally. Although traffic between Asia and North America is increasing fast, the biggest traffic flow in the world between regions is between Europe and North America.

30%
Internally

70%
USA and Canada

Latin America and the Caribbean
Between 2006 and 2010, this region's international Internet traffic grew by approximately 71 per cent each year. At the current time, most of its data travels between the countries in the region, or to North America before being routed to other regions around the world.

Africa
Africa is the continent with the smallest fraction of its people online (less than 9.5 per cent). Few African cities boast the capacity of cities in other regions. New cables are being laid to increase Africa's capacity but with people spread over great distances, wireless technologies may be more effective.

6%
USA and Canada

11%
Asia-Pacific

1%
Internally

82%
Europe

Miami gateway

Some 90 per cent of all Internet traffic between North America and Latin America goes through one building in downtown Miami, USA. The Terremark data centre is an Internet exchange filled with thousands of server computers. They are protected by round-the-clock security and 18-cm (7-in) thick walls capable of withstanding a hurricane.

Did you know?

More than 160 different cable networks meet and run through the Terremark building in Miami. On its roof are mounted two 16 m (52-ft) and one 14 m (46 ft) satellite dishes.

Seat of learning

Famous for its technical and scientific innovation, Stanford University in Palo Alto, Santa Clara Valley, was formed in 1891 and established the Stanford Research Institute (SRI) in 1946 to build technology ties with local business. Many Silicon Valley legends would pass through either the university or SRI before forming their own start-ups.

← Hewlett Packard (H
In 1938, two Stanford engineering graduates, B Hewlett and Dave Packar began work in this garag in Palo Alto. HP is now or of the largest information technology companies.

Silicon Valley

It all started here. A stretch of Californian land, south of San Francisco, USA, became home to the greatest concentration of computing and high-tech pioneers ever known. Named Silicon Valley, after the material that is used in computer electronics, the HQs of many huge Internet and computing companies are found in the area.

← Intel
Intel was founded by three former Fairchild engineers in 1968 to build memory chips. By 1992, Intel was the world's largest semiconductor company, famous for supplying the processor chips inside IBM PCs.

Orchards to Apple Inc

Once full of apple orchards and known as "The Valley of Heart's Delight", the Silicon Valley region includes the Santa Clara Valley and the city of San Jose. In the 1950s, several high-technology companies moved their research bases to the area, and a group of engineers formed Fairchild Semiconductor, which pioneered computer-circuit technology. By 1972, more than 60 electronics companies were based in the valley, most formed by ex-Fairchild employees. Four years later, Apple made its base here, too.

← SanDisk
In 1988, the memory card and USB flash drive giant, SanDisk, was founded by an Israeli scientist and a former Intel employee in Silicon Valley.

← Facebook
Facebook began as a social networking site used by students of Harvard University, on the east coast of the USA. In 2004, it moved west and made its HQ in Palo Alto.

SanDisk
Headquarters

PARC →
In 1970, Xerox opened the Palo Alto Research Center (PARC), a high-tech research and development base. Optical discs, laser printing, and user interfaces, such as Windows, all first came from this Silicon Valley-based think tank.

Symantec →
Gary Hendrix worked at SRI before founding a company that became Symantec, the makers of Norton AntiVirus amongst other popular computer software. They are based in Mountain View, a stone's throw away from Google's HQ.

parc
Palo Alto Research Center
3333 COYOTE HILL ROAD

Symantec
World Headquarters

Adobe →
Adobe was formed in 1982 by two PARC researchers who developed the postscript printer language. Seven years later, Adobe released the image-editing software, Photoshop. In 1993, Adobe introduced the famous PDF file format.

Adobe

Heavy hitters

Dozens of high-tech companies have bases in Silicon Valley, from Adobe to Yahoo! This is partly due to ex-employees of one company forming their own nearby, such as former Apple employee Trip Hawkins, who went on to found Electronic Arts, one of the first home computer game companies, in 1982.

YAHOO!

← Yahoo!
In 1994, two Stanford University students created a website named David and Jerry's Guide to the World Wide Web. This became Yahoo!, which made a profit of £368 million (US$598) million in 2009.

SUN Microsystems →
1982, SUN (named after the Stanford University Network) began by making computers. In 1995, SUN produced the Java computer language, now one of the most widely used computer programming languages.

Sun
microsystems

Buildings
15, 16
Sun Learning Services

4150, 4160
Network Circle

eBay →
Pierre Omidyar was working as a software engineer in Silicon Valley when he began the Internet-auction website at his home in San Jose. eBay's HQ remains in the city.

ebay

"I think it's fair to say that personal computers have become the most empowering tool we've ever created. They're tools of communication, they're tools of creativity, and they can be shaped by their user."

Bill Gates

American Bill Gates (born 1955) is the co-founder and chairman of Microsoft, the world's largest software company. He began programming as a teenager and dropped out of university to form Microsoft in 1975. Ten years later the company launched the first version of Windows, the operating system now installed on more than 85 per cent of all desktop and notebook computers. Gates is one of the world's wealthiest people and in 1994 set up a charitable organization to which he has donated more than £20 billion (US$28 billion). The Bill and Melinda Gates Foundation is dedicated to bringing innovation in health, development, and learning in the global community.

Did you know?

Bill Gates has a fly named after him, in recognition of his contribution to Dipterology, the science of flies. *Eristalis gatesi* is a species of flower fly that lives in the forests of Costa Rica.

How Apple grew

Founded by Steve Jobs, Steve Wozniak, and Ronald Wayne on 1 April 1976, Apple has grown from a tiny start-up in a California bedroom to a global brand that employs more than 46,000 people. In 2010, the company boasted profits of £9.5 billion (US$14 billion). Famous for their design and innovation, Apple products have helped revolutionize the computing, music, and phone industries.

Did you know?
The Apple Lisa, regarded as Apple's largest commercial failure, was named after Steve Jobs' daughter. It went on sale for a whopping £6,300 (US$10,000)!

← 1984, Macintosh 128K
A 23-cm (9-in) black-and-white screen was built into the first Apple Mac, which went on sale for £1,800 (US$2,495).

→ 1997, Power Mac G3
Found in tests to be faster than rival PCs, the Power Mac was advertised on TV using snails and rabbits.

↓ 1999, iBook
A range of colourful laptops launched with organic, clamshell-shaped cases and built-in handles.

↓ 1976, First Apple computer
Only 200 Apple Is were ever built, and now they're collectors' items. They cost £325 (US$666.66) new, but in 2010, one sold at auction for £120,000 (US$178,000).

↓ 1991, PowerBook 100
Weighing just over 2 kg (4 lb), the slimmed down PowerBook 100 was Apple's first successful portable computer.

↓ 1997, 20th Anniversary Mac
This unusual machine included a Bose sound system and built-in TV and radio. Its price tag was £6,125 (US$10,000).

↑ 1987, Macintosh 2
With its separate hard drive, screen, and keyboard, this was the first modular Mac.

↓ 1999, AirPort
A Wi-Fi base station that created a wireless local area network for Apple computers to connect to the Internet.

↑ 1977, Apple II
The first successful home computer with colour graphics. Versions of the Apple II would be sold new until 1993.

↘ 1989, Mac Portable
Apple's first portable computer weighed almost 7 kg (15 lb) and was a commercial flop.

↘ 1998, iMac
The Apple iMac G3 was released in 13 different colours, including Bondi Blue, Sage, Ruby, Grape, and Blue Dalmatian.

← 1982, Apple Lisa
The first Apple with a mouse and graphical user interface (GUI), the Lisa had a 5 MB external hard disk.

↑ 1994, Power Macintosh 8100
The range of fast Power Macintoshes was produced up until 2006.

↑ 1999, Power Mac G4
Codenamed "Yikes!" during development, this machine was one of the first PCs with a recordable DVD drive.

Steve Jobs and Steve Wozniak

Twelve days after co-founding Apple, Ronald Wayne sold his 10-per-cent share for just £430 (US$800) (it would now be worth billions). The two Steves led Apple through its early years. Wozniak (right) stopped working full-time for Apple in 1987, but is still on the payroll. Jobs (left) left in 1984 to buy and run Pixar, but returned to head Apple in the late 1990s.

"Do you want to spend the rest of your life selling sugared water or do you want a chance to change the world?"

Steve Jobs to John Sculley (at centre of picture left), then CEO of Pepsi, trying to convince him to join Apple

↑ 2001, PowerBook G4
The first in a series of slimline laptops with a front-loading DVD slot and a 38-cm (15-in) screen.

↗ 2001, First iPod
The iPod launched with a 4-cm (1.5-in) hard disk able to hold up to 1,000 tracks, but was compatible only with Apple computers.

↑ 2002, The New iMac
The successor to the original iMac had a 38-cm (15-in) colour screen and an unusual, domed body.

↑ 2006, Wireless Mighty Mouse
Apple's first multi-button mouse came complete with a small internal speaker in its shell.

↓ 2006, MacBook
The first in a line of MacBook laptops that will become Apple's biggest selling family of computers.

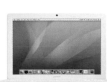

↑ 2007, iPhone
Following years of speculation, Apple's first touchscreen-enabled smartphone went on sale. The 8 GB model cost £300 (US$599).

↑ 2008, MacBook
This revised MacBook came with an aluminium case and a giant touch pad.

2009, iPhone 3GS
Two years after the first iPhone, the third generation arrived with more speed, 32 GB of memory, and a video camera.

↑ 2010, iPad
A tablet computer particularly suited to viewing multimedia apps on its multi-touch 25-cm (9.8-in) screen, is launched.

↗ 2009, iPod Touch
Half-iPod and half-iPhone (but without voice calls), the iPod Touch has up to 64GB of internal storage.

2010, iPhone 4
Apple's fourth version of the iPhone featured a new steel and glass frame, and a new "retina" display allowing ultra sharp text and images.

↓ 2000, G4 Cube
An unusual, cube-shaped desktop computer with a clear acrylic outer body, the G4 Cube is still in demand for use as a fish tank or "Mac-quarium".

↘ 2003, Power Mac G5
Eleven hundred of these high performance machines were linked together to form the System X supercomputer cluster at Virginia Tech University, USA.

↘ 2007, iMac
Completely restyled iMacs with slim aluminium bodies were released in 50 cm (20-in) and 60-cm (24 in) screen versions.

↑ 2008, MacBook Air
Just 4 mm (0.2 in) thick in places, with a body made from one sheet of aluminium, the Air was the first Apple to offer solid-state storage.

↘ 2009, Magic Mouse
This wireless mouse was the first to feature multi-touch sensing (as used on the iPhone).

↓ 2010, Apple TV
This update to the Apple TV released in 1997 connects to a TV, allowing users to stream video and music from iTunes, YouTube, and elsewhere.

What's behind a website?

A website is a collection of documents called web pages, which contain text, images, and links to other web pages. Most websites are created using a code called Hypertext Markup Language (HTML). There is software that sets up a website structure to which the user adds text and images.

Language of the Web

HTML was developed by British Web pioneer, Tim Berners-Lee and, with revisions, is still the most common way to format text and images to form a web page. HTML provides a wide range of coded commands, known as tags, that allow users to format text, insert photos, graphics, or multimedia files, and build tables of information. Links must also be established between the website's own pages.

What else do you need?

Once you have a website you need a web hosting company to store it on a server, making it available 24/7. You also need an Internet connection to upload your pages to the server and a name. This consists of a top-level domain name, after the dot, such as **.com** and your website title.

What is a blog?

The term "blog" comes from "web log" – a space online used like a diary or journal to post up messages. It is easy to start a blog. They are often part of a regular website, and there are also dedicated blogging site hosts. All you have to do is sign up. Blogs are regularly updated and most are interactive, allowing visitors to leave comments.

Browsers

A web browser is an application that gives you access to the Web. It translates HTML tags to display web pages on your computer. This laptop screen (right) displays a website homepage and the HTML code used to create it. For a website to reach as many people as possible, its pages must be compatible with all the most popular browsers.

Finder   File   Edit   View   Go

Selecting "view source" in a browser reveals the HTML code

```
</HEAD>

<script language="j
src="http://us.pengu
</script>

<script language="Ja
src="http://us.pengu
>
```

The web page's main content begins here

```
<body>
```

This code tells the website which image to display

```
<!-- main content ar
<div id="container">
<!-- header -->
<div id="header"><h1
width="122" height="
</div>
<!-- end header -->
<p>Click on a flag t
<div class="clear">

<!-- flags  -->
<!--flags row 1 -->
<div class="flagsect
uk.co.uk" onClick="r
uk.html'+redirectStr
src="images/uk_flag.
United Kingdom</a></
<div class="flagsect
```

Instructs the browser to open a new window

```
onClick="newindow('c
usa.html'+redirectSt
src="images/us_flag.
United States</a></a

<div class="flagsect
onClick="newindow('c
canada.html'+redirec
src="images/ca_flag.
  Canada</a></div>
<div class="flagsect
onClick="newindow('c
australia.html'+redi
src="images/au_flag.
  Australia</a></div
<div class="flagsect
href="http://www.dor
```

Images are hyperlinked to another web page

```
onClick="newindow('c
germany.html'+redire
src="images/ge_flag.
  Germany</a></div>
```

//dk.com/

```
tic/misc/us/mainscript.js">

tic/misc/all/commonjs.js"></script

es/dk_logo.gif" alt="DK"
</h1>

n country</p>

ttp://www.dorlingkindersley-
', 'choose-
n false;"><img
ag" /><br />

ttp://us.penguingroup.com"
rn false;"><img
ag" /><br />

ttp://cn.dk.com"
eturn false;"><img
ian flag" /><br />

ttp://www.penguin.com.au/dk"
);return false;"><img
alia flag" /><br />

erlag.de"

return false;"><img
n flag" /><br />
```

Firefox

Website address, or domain name

Flags act as hyperlinks, (active links) taking you to a new web page

Did you know?

By the end of 2010, there were an estimated 255 million websites worldwide. The number of web pages is in the trillions.

Dorling Kindersley – Illustrated Reference Publisher

http://www.dk.com →

Search engine

Dorling Kindersley

 www.dk.com

Click on a flag to visit a chosen country

United Kingdom

United States

Canada

Australia

India

South Africa

China

Spain

© 2011 Dorling Kindersley™ Limited

What do search engines do?

The Internet is beyond enormous. Thousands of millions of web pages, many of which are unhelpfully entitled "page 1" or "home", sit on web servers that also have technical or cryptic names and are impossible to find by yourself. Search engines cut through all of this complexity to provide you with a series of results to your requests for information. Their value and importance to Internet users has rocketed, turning the most successful into enormous businesses, handling vast amounts of data. In 1998, Google handled around 10,000 search queries per day. In 2010, that figure had risen to more than 1,000 million.

↖ Baidu

Founded in 2000 by Robin Li and Eric Xu, Baidu is a Chinese language search engine that continues to grow. Google spotted its potential in 2005 when it offered to buy it for £993 million (US$1,600 million) and was turned down. Baidu now indexes more than 740 million web pages and is responsible for 73 per cent of search requests made in China.

- Baidu makes its money from advertising, including a system where advertisers bid to get their ads and links placed alongside certain search results. It has proven successful – Baidu made a £372 million (US$599 million) profit in 2010.

- "Search is a highly competitive game. For a user to leave us and go to somebody else, it's just one click." Kaiser Kuo, a Baidu spokesperson, 2010.

新闻 网页 贴吧 知道 MP3 图片 视频 地图

空间 百科 hao123 | 更多>>

百度一下 | 输入法 ☐

加入百度推广 | 搜索风云榜 | 关于百度 | About Baidu
©2011 Baidu 使用百度前必读 京ICP证030173号 ⬡

○○○
◀ ▶ | ▲ ▼ | ⟳ | + | http://www.whatdosearchenginesdo.com ↦

What do search engines do? ↦

What do search engines do? – Search engine

Ask Google Bing Yahoo! Baidu AOL Monster.com TinEye Seznam Naver News ↦

Web | Images | Videos | Maps | Shopping | Mail | More ↦

Web history | Settings ↦ | Chat | Mail | Sign out

Search engine

What do search engines do?

Search

About 240,000,000 results | 0.10 seconds |

Advance search

Everything
Images
Videos
News
Shopping
Realtime
More →

Engine explosion

Before the World Wide Web, there were still search engines that looked for names of files available over the Internet. One of the first, and best known is Archie, created by Canadian student Alan Emtage in 1990. The mid-to-late 1990s saw a battle between search's big beasts, including AltaVista, Lycos, Infoseek, Magellan, and Yahoo!, before Google rose to prominence.

Cached | Similar

Archie Query Form

Search for: 🔍

Search Engine Share

Worldwide, Google dominates the search engine market to a spectacular extent. In January 2011, NetMarketShare reported that whilst Yahoo! had 6.14, Bing 3.68, and Baidu 2.92 per cent of global market share, Google's search engines accounted for 85.37 per cent. In a handful of countries, however, locally produced search engines still outrank Google. These include Naver in South Korea and Yandex in Russia, whilst in the Czech Republic, Google is locked in an ongoing battle with Seznam.cz to be number one.

When you type in search keywords to a search engine, your request is sent to the engine's index, which seeks out matches amongst its masses of data, orders them according to their rank (see below), and then returns search engine results pages. All of this happens in a fraction of a second.

Cached | Similar

Web crawling

A search request accesses an enormous body of data stored on a search engine's index servers. These indexes are compiled using automated computer scripts called crawlers. These crawl through the entire World Wide Web scouring web pages and sending back their results to the index.

Cached | Similar

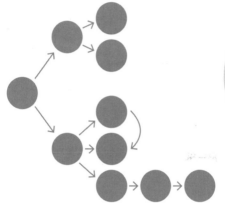

Search algorithms

The data in an index server is stored as a form of database. Each search engine uses a different method to search for a user's keyword using a set of search rules called an algorithm. These are highly complex and involve dozens or sometimes hundreds of different elements. Search algorithms tend to be closely guarded trade secrets.

Cached | Similar

Ranking pages

Whatever the algorithm used, all search engines seek to rank web pages in order of their relevance to the search the user has requested. They do this by looking for the search keywords featuring throughout each web page, but give greater weight to them occurring in the title of the web page or in its headings. They also count the frequency with which the keyword appears on the page to assess how relevant the page is to the search.

Cached | Similar

Did you know?

Users of the Midomi search engine can sing, hum, or whistle a tune into their phone or computer and it will try to match the sounds to the music stored in its index.

Off the page

Many search engines perform off-page analysis of a web page, mainly looking at its links to other websites, their number, quality, and popularity, helping the search engine to determine the importance of the page.

Search Engine Optimization (SEO)

There is fierce competition to make it to the front page of search results, especially in common subjects such as music or shopping that may already be populated by thousands of rival websites. SEO experts use a variety of techniques including adjusting a web page's keywords and title, and fostering links to strong websites. Some also use black hat techniques – these frowned-upon methods include keyword stuffing (adding lots of popular keywords to a web page that aren't relevant) and link farms (where hundreds of websites all link to every other web page) trying to give them a boost in the rankings.

"The ultimate search engine would basically understand everything in the world and it would always give you the right thing. And we're a long, long way from that."

Larry Page, co-founder and CEO of Google

Did you know?

Launched in 1998, UFOSeek.com is a search engine dedicated to UFOs, aliens, and other unexplained phenomena.

EZRAM

Apply now →

Compare all sites

Apply now →

Compare all sites

← → 🏠 + http://www.google.co.uk/ ↻ Q▾

www. google.com

Web Images Videos Maps News Shopping Gmail more ▼ | iGoogle | Settings ▼ | Sign out

Google

Who invented Google?

Google Search   I'm feeling lucky

In 1995, 22-year-old Larry Page was shown around Stanford University, USA, by another student, Sergey Brin. The two disagreed on pretty much everything. However, the next year, when they ended up working together on a new search engine called BackRub, the two of them got on better. They also hit upon a winning formula that would soon become Google, the world's most popular search engine. In 2009, *Forbes* business magazine described Page and Brin as the fifth most powerful people in the world.

PageRank

Early search engines ranked web pages by how often the search term appeared on the page. Page and Brin's PageRank system used in Google went far further. It analysed the number, quality, and importance of other pages that linked to that web page to produce more accurate and useful search results. Today, PageRank is just one of more than 200 different factors that enable most Google searches to be fast, accurate, and relevant.

Sergey Brin →
Sergey's father was a mathematics professor and his mother was a space scientist. He was born in Moscow but left Russia for the USA at the age of six. Brin has donated more than £2.5 million (US$4 million) to a space tourism company.

Larry Page →
Larry's parents were both computer science professors. Whilst studying computer science himself at the University of Michigan, USA, Page built an inkjet plotter-printer out of Lego bricks. He and Brin co-own a Boeing 767 aircraft as well as two business jets.

Growing fast

Brin and Page renamed BackRub "Google" in 1997 and the following year formed a company. At first, they operated out of a friend's garage in Menlo Park, California (below), but Google grew quickly. In 2000, Brin and Page released 10 foreign language versions. In 2002, this grew to 72, one of which was Klingon, the fictional language from *Star Trek*. By this time, Google's search index of more than a billion web pages made it the largest in the world.

Reader →

Branching out

In order to stay ahead of rivals and attract valuable advertising, Google continued to add new features, including news, book, and image searches. Google Maps arrived in 2005, while Google Chrome is one of the top two web browsers (applications that give you access to the information on the Web) in many countries. Not all Google's projects have been resounding successes. Google Answers, Google Lively (a 3-D virtual world), and Google Wave (a social networking site) didn't attract enough of a following and were shut down.

You Tube →

The Googleplex

Google has offices in more than 50 locations, but its HQ is in Mountain View, California, USA. Long hours and hard work are part of Googleplex life, but there's plenty of fun to be had as well. There are weekly roller hockey matches in the car park, and the buildings also boast a gym, two swimming pools, pool tables, beach volleyball courts, a giant dinosaur skeleton, more than a dozen cafés, and even an adult-sized rubber ball pit.

Chrome ↑

"Don't be evil!"

The informal motto of Google, which aims to be successful while always doing the right thing.

Blogger ↑

Google Earth →

- An estimated 80 to 85 per cent of all queries on the Internet are typed into Google's search engines, and google.com is the most visited website in the world.

- According to ComScore in 2010, 34,000 searches are made on Google every second. That's about 88 billion searches a month.

- The first doodle (above) livened up Google's sparse home page in 1998. Now, an entire team is responsible for the Google doodles.

- Google makes its money from advertising, helping to direct web users (traffic) to advertisers' websites. In 2009, advertisers paid Google £15.5 billion (US$22.9 billion).

- Since 2001, Google has bought more than 80 companies, including YouTube, Blogger, photo-sharing site Picasa, and slide.com.

- In 1999, Brin and Page offered Google to a rival company, Excite, for just £680,000 (US$1 million). Excite turned down the offer.

- Google strives to be eco-friendly. Solar panels generate up to 30 per cent of the Googleplex's electricity and, each year, goats are brought in to "mow" the grass.

- Brin and Page pay themselves just 68p (US$1) a year – but their Google shares make them billionaires.

- "Google" is a play on *googol*, which means 1 followed by 100 zeroes.

Gmail ↑

20-per-cent time

Google allows its employees to spend up to a fifth of their working week on special pet projects. Brin and Page believe that if an engineer is passionate about a project, it has the best chance of being a success. Google News, the Orkut social networking site, and Gmail, which has more than 146 million users, are three successful applications created by Google staff using 20-per-cent time.

Images →

Server farm

A server is a computer that handles files, tasks and data from other computers, known as clients. A server farm is a collection of computer servers all in one location. Server farms can perform a wide range of tasks from storing companies' computer data securely to hosting websites and transmitting data over the Internet. Large quantities of data can flow to and from the server farm and the businesses and organizations that are its customers.

Did you know?

Most companies keep their server details secret, though the web hosting company 1&1 Internet admits it uses more than 70,000 servers. No one knows for sure, but it is estimated that Google runs a million servers worldwide.

The Pionen facility

In 2007 and 2008, more than 4,000 cu m (140,000 cu ft) of solid rock were blasted away to turn this former nuclear bunker into a server farm. It covers an area of 1,110 sq m (12,000 sq ft).

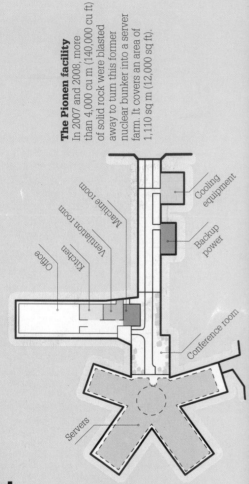

Office

Kitchen

Ventilation room

Machine room

Cooling equipment

Backup power

Conference room

Servers

Super server

Some 30 m (100 ft) below the city of Stockholm is a bunker hewn out of granite rock. The Pionen data centre belongs to Bahnhof, one of Sweden's biggest Internet service providers. Secured behind its 40-cm- (16-in-) thick steel doors, more than 6,000 computer servers shift millions of bytes of data over computer networks.

World apart

The Pionen data centre features lamps that simulate daylight, large numbers of plants, artificial waterfalls, and a giant, 2,600-litre (570-gallon) saltwater fish tank. The floor of its conference room is a replica of the Moon's surface.

Cooling issues

Electricity is one of a server farm's biggest expenses. It is needed both to power the machines and to keep them cool. At the Pionen data centre, two giant diesel engines from a German submarine power the generators (pictured) that provide backup electricity. The server farm has a warning system in case there is a security breach or a major technical fault with a group of servers. This consists of loud horns from the same submarine.

Our time online

People spend their time online in a vast number of different ways. Some use their time to learn about a subject in depth while others prefer skimming through lots of different topics, picking up snippets and facts along the way. Many people get involved in online communities dedicated to particular hobbies or interests, from supporting the same sports team to sharing their passion for vintage cars or photography, or experiences of owning a pet. Whatever their interests, most people tend to use the Internet for many different purposes throughout a single day.

Did you know?

In 2007, the small European nation of Estonia became the first country to offer online voting in its national parliamentary elections.

Really Simple Syndication (RSS)

It wasn't that long ago that the only way to keep track of updates on your favourite website was to find it in your web browser, again and again. RSS or Really Simple Syndication automates the process for you by sending headlines and summaries of updates and new content from websites you subscribe to. New material is sent out to you automatically as it is posted online.

cafe

Social networking

Keeping in touch with friends through jokes, banter, and games, finding old friends, and making new ones are part of the appeal of social networking sites like Facebook, MySpace, and Bebo. Still growing in popularity, new apps, games, and quizzes, especially on Facebook, are seeing people spend more and more time online, social networking.

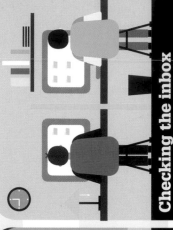

Checking the inbox

Millions of people start their working day by checking their email inbox, whether they are travelling, in the office, or working from home. An estimated 2.8 million emails are sent every second by the world's 1.9 billion email users, many of whom have more than one account. Email numbers are increased further by junk emails known as spam.

Off to work

Millions of people have long journeys using public transport to and from work. These commuters are well-served by technologies designed for use on the move, from media players with headphones that cancel out much of the background noise, to smartphones capable of picking up emails or displaying web pages.

Morning news

Grabbing the morning news used to be a simple matter of waiting for the newspaper to be delivered or switching on the radio. Now, many cannot resist starting the day by powering up their laptop or PC to read the latest headlines online. Some head direct to a particular news agency or media site whilst others use RSS feeds (above).

Working from home

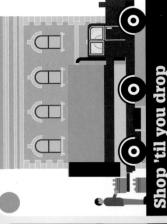

Many people now work for companies from home, accessing company information and contacting co-workers via an Internet connection. The Internet has helped thousands of people to start their own businesses, getting advice, contacts, and even funding from online sources, and gaining orders and work via their websites.

Blogging

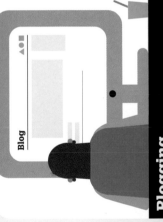

Lots of people like to share their opinions with others online. Newspaper and other media websites encourage readers' comments as they help keep people on their sites for longer and generate additional content for free. Blogs contain a person's thoughts, views, and stories as well as links to other blogs or websites.

Money matters

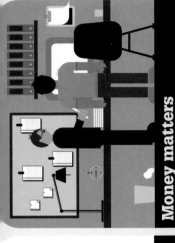

More and more people handle their personal finances online, enjoying the convenience of online banking and trusting in the security layers and encryption software employed by banks to protect their accounts. Others invest via online shares dealing, while financial news updates allow people to keep track of financial markets all over the world.

Shop 'til you drop

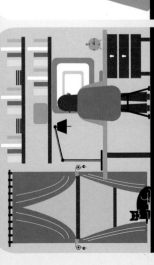

E-commerce has proved very popular with customers, who are able to find and buy goods from all over the world via international shopping sites. Shoppers take advantage of price comparison websites to get the best price, scour the net for discount vouchers, and can look up online reviews of products.

Face to face

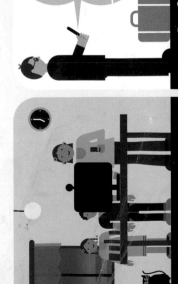

A webcam, either built into or attached to a monitor or laptop screen, allows images to be sent and received, keeping people in touch, face to face. Video conferencing means a meeting can be held in different locations at the same time, while video relay services enable people to communicate with sign language over the Internet through an interpreter.

Face the facts

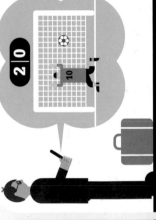

Up to the minute access to facts, scores, and updates has become essential for many people. Now equipped with easy-to-use websearches by voice on some smartphones or by keyword on e-readers, tablets, and PCs. Celebrity gossip websites, and sports update services, that offer results and news are particularly popular.

Evening entertainment

An evening in with the laptop might involve a mixture of emails, social networking, and catching up on TV shows using video sites like Hulu, on which Americans watch 924 million videos per month, or YouTube, which has 12.2 billion video clips viewed every month. You can also access movie streaming websites and download music.

Late-night gaming

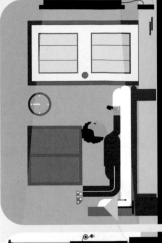

Gaming is popular at all hours with many Internet users, who enjoy the range of highly addictive games on offer. The evening is often a good time for more involved gaming, for competing with players around the world, or for using forums to share and swap tips and tricks, including cheats to games.

Social networking

Keeping in touch with friends, known as social networking, now occupies more of people's time online than any other activity. Statistics for June 2010 saw social networking sites like Bebo, MySpace, and Facebook account for 22.7 per cent of all time spent on the Web in the USA. In contrast, Americans spend 10.2 per cent of their time on online games, 8.3 per cent on emails, and 3.9 per cent watching videos.

Facebook facts

In 2010, the largest social networking site, Facebook, boasted more than **500 million** members.

Top 5 countries on Facebook in 2010

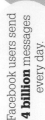

Country	Users
France	20,307,260
Turkey	23,823,200
UK	28,770,560
Indonesia	31,425,840
USA	145,331,600

In 2010, every month the average Facebook user created **90** pieces of content, from uploaded photos to messages.

Facebook users send **4 billion** messages every day.

Thanks to some **300,000** Facebook users who helped provide translations, Facebook is now available in 70 different languages including

Networking nations

According to one survey, in 2010 the nations with the highest percentage of Internet users active on at least one social networking site were:

Brazil – **95%**

USA – **84%**

Portugal – **82%**

BOOM!

Globally, there was an **82.2%** increase in the time spent on social networking sites between December 2008 and December 2009.

Turn it off!

According to a 2010 study, **48%** of social networkers confessed they update or check Twitter or Facebook after having gone to bed or first thing in the morning.

Silver surfers

Social networking was once thought only a young person's game. Now, everyone is getting in on the act. In early 2010, statistics showed that **47% of 50–64-year-old Internet users** surf social networking sites. And **26%** of users **over 60** use the Internet to social network.

Watch the time

The average visitor to a social network site spent **66%** more time on such sites in 2010 than they did a year earlier.

Twitter

The social networking site Twitter allows you to follow microblogs from friends and celebrities.

A Twitter message, with a maximum of **140 characters**, is called a tweet. On average, **95 million tweets** are written every day.

In October 2010, there were 175 million Twitter users. An estimated **300,000** new users sign up each day to send and receive tweets.

In January 2010, whilst onboard the International Space Station, astronaut T J Creamer sent the first Twitter message from space.

Hollywood actor, Ashton Kutcher is a super-keen tweeter. Up to December 2010, he had sent **6,368** tweets.

In 2010, the most popular person on Twitter was US pop singer Lady Gaga, with **7,252,223** followers.

English is the most popular language on Facebook, with **213.2 million** users – **52.2%** of total users. Next is Spanish **(61.2 million)**, French **(23.5 million)**, Turkish **(21.9 million)**, and Indonesian **(20.5 million)**.

Facebook continues to grow rapidly. In October 2010 alone, an additional **2,974,000** Indonesians joined up along with **1.66 million** Mexicans, and **1.56 million** new users from India.

Every month about **290 million** Facebook users log on just to play games.

The majority of Facebook gamers – a surprising **69%** – are women.

With more than **75 million** registered players, *FarmVille* is the biggest Facebook game of all. Players plant, tend, and harvest virtual crops.

Around the world

Mixi
Japan's biggest social network, Mixi, began in 2004 and has around **16 million** users. Fewer than **5%** of members use their real name or photos, preferring anonymity.

Ibibo
Indian social networking site Ibibo, short for iBuild, iBond, has more than **3.5 million** users and receives more than **51 million** page views per day.

VKontakt
With more than **98 million** members, VKontakte is Russia's largest social networking site and second most visited website.

Qzone
China's largest social networking site, Qzone, has **150 million** users who update their accounts at least once a month. Instant messaging remains the favourite way of social networking in China. Qzone's QQ instant messenger service attracts **40–50 million** users at any one time.

Orkut
Named after its creator, Google employee Orkut Büyükkökten, social networking site Orkut has **100 million** regular users. In April 2010, **48%** of Orkut's users were from Brazil, **39.2%** from India, and **2.2%** from the USA.

Out of space?

Until the boom of Facebook, MySpace was the biggest social networking site in the world. The **100-millionth MySpace account** was created on August 2006 in the **Netherlands**.

PHOTO FUN

In September 2010, Flickr, the social networking website designed for sharing photos and videos, held **5 billion images**.

Down and out?

Not all social networking sites are booming. Bebo, short for Blog Early, Blog Often, was sold by AOL in 2010 after its number of users fell by as much as **50%** in a year. AOL paid **£530 million** (US$850 million) for Bebo, but according to reports, sold it for just **£6 million** (US$10 million).

NO GO

10 In 2006, global shopping chain Wal-Mart set up its own online social networking site for teens called The Hub. It required parental consent to use and was considered too full of adverts. It survived just **10 weeks**.

people: it will be shared among the millions of connections people have."

Mark Zuckerberg

Mark Zuckerberg (born 1984) is the originator of social networking monster, Facebook. The site grew out of Facemash, which allowed students at Harvard University, USA, to rate pictures of each other. Zuckerberg and three friends launched Facebook from their dormitory rooms in 2004, and had a million users within 10 months. The story of Facebook's creation was the subject of a movie, The Social Network (2010). Zuckerberg still heads Facebook and is said to have turned down takeover offers from Yahoo!, Viacom, and Microsoft among others. In January 2011, Facebook was valued at more than £30 billion (US$50 billion).

Did you know?

The styling of Facebook's website is predominantly blue. This is because Zuckerberg has red–green colour blindness and sees the colour blue best.

The growth of the Web

The World Wide Web is exploding in size. From a barely noticeable handful of websites 20 years ago, it has mushroomed into a gigantic resource. In 2010 alone, some 21.4 million new websites were added to the Web. And as huge countries like China, India, Indonesia, and Brazil get more and more of their population online, it is only set to get bigger and bigger.

Top 20

The top 20 countries in the world with the most Internet users make up for three quarters of all Internet users (75.8%) and number almost 1.5 billion. China has the most Internet users of any country in the world – 420 million and rising.

Did you know?

Between 2003 and 2009, the average size of a webpage increased by 400% as more features and images were included.

North America
266,224,500
77.4%

Europe
475,069,448
58.4%

Asia
825,094,396
21.5%

Middle East
63,240,946
29.8%

Africa
110,931,700
10.9%

Latin America/Caribbean
204,689,836
34.5%

Oceania / Australia
21,272,470
61.3%

Did you know?

Access to the Internet is considered a legal right in Finland, Estonia, and Spain.

↑ World statistics

The Internet has not penetrated evenly across the world. The figures above show first the number of Internet users in each region in 2010, and then give this as a percentage of the total population.

Number of websites

1993	1994	1995	1996	2009
130	2,738	23,500	230,000	215,675,903

The number of individual web pages now numbers in the trillions.

Number of worldwide Internet users

2000	2010
360,985,492	1,966,514,816

That's a growth of
448.8%

In 2010, the global percentage of people with Internet access was 28.7%.

Countries with the most Internet users:

 China
420,000,000

 USA
239,893,600

 Japan
99,143,700

India
81,000,000

Brazil
75,943,600

Most visited websites
Google publishes a list of the number of monthly unique visitors the world's other most popular websites receive. While the exact number remains a mystery for Google itself, it's safe to assume that they would top this list.

facebook 590,000,000

YouTube 490,000,000

YAHOO! UK 450,000,000

Windows Live 340,000,000

WIKIPEDIA 310,000,000

Haves and have nots
There's a big difference between the populations of developed nations with access to the Internet and those of developing nations.

The name game
The domain name of a website (the letters after the dot at the end of the address) tell you a lot about it – for example, whether it is a government (**.gov**) or educational (**.edu**) organization, or the country of the website's origin (**.fr** for France).

- The tiny Pacific island nation of Tuvalu (population 11,600) received a windfall from 2000 onwards when it sold its right to its **.tv** domain names particularly to tv channels.

- Two other countries with domains sought-after by radio stations are:
.fm - Federated states of Micronesia
.am - Armenia

What are we doing?
Below are the top activities we do online, the percentage of daily users, and the average amount of time they spend on the activity per week.

Email 72% of users send email
4.4 hours average per week

News 55% check news
2.7 hours average per week

Social 46% social network
4.6 hours average per week

Interest 46% pursue interests online
3.9 hours average per week

Knowledge 39% look up information
3.1 hours average per week

Multimedia 37% watch films or tv
3.7 hours average per week

Gaming 27% play games
2.9 hours average per week

Browsing 24% browse generally
2.3 hours average per week

Admin 21% do personal admin
1.7 hours spent per week

Organize 19% plan their lives online
1.6 hours average per week

Shopping 12% shop online
1.8 hours average per week

Top languages used on the Web

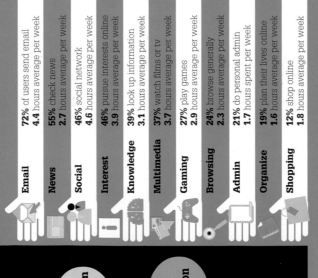

English 536.56 million
Chinese 444.95 million
Spanish 153.31 million
Japanese 99.14 million
Portuguese 65.36 million
German 75.16 million
Arabic 65.36 million
French 59.78 million
Russian 59.7 million
Korean 39.44 million

Haves and have nots

Developed nations **71%**

Developing nations **21%**

The top three countries that have the highest percentage of population with Internet access are:

Iceland **97.6%**

Norway **94.9%**

Sweden **92.5%**

The countries with lowest Internet access are:

Myanmar **0.2%**

East Timor **0.1%**

Access all areas

Imagine facing a 2-day trek every time you wanted to check your email. That is the prospect facing many who live in rural parts of mountainous Nepal. Here, on the "Roof of the World", fewer than 3 per cent of the country's 29 million people have direct Internet access. Nepal is far from alone. There is a huge digital divide between the Internet haves and have-nots around the world. All sorts of initiatives, both big and small, are working to shrink the gap.

Mahabir Pun
Returning home to Nepal after studying in the USA, Mahabir Pun built a wireless connection between his village and its neighbours in 2001, using an old TV satellite dish. Since then, Pun has helped to bring Internet access to more than 100 Nepalese villages, using donated old PCs and parts.

Did you know?

According to Internet World Stats in 2010, more than three-quarters of the US population were Internet users. By contrast, just 0.3 per cent of the population of the African nation of Sierra Leone used the Internet.

Network Nepal

Many communities in rural Nepal are remote, at high altitude, cut off by steep valleys, and poorly served by roads or electricity. Building long-distance Wi-Fi networks in this terrain has been a huge challenge. Materials have been carried up by hand to construct the relay towers that beam the signal through the narrow valleys. The highest tower stands 3,600 m (11,800 ft) above sea level and is manned by a yak farmer, who must check the connections every day.

Online impact

The Internet has brought together isolated Nepalese communities. Schoolchildren work online, farmers can buy and sell on a local trading website, and healthworkers use webcams so patients can be examined by hospital doctors in the capital, Kathmandu.

Everest 3G

In 2010, the Nepalese telecoms company Ncell brought wireless 3G Internet and phone coverage to Mount Everest – its climbers, guides, and nearby villages. As there is no electricity supply, the system's 10 base stations are powered by solar panels, with batteries for backup. The highest of the stations is 5,200 m (17,060 ft) above sea level.

How the Web is run

The World Wide Web is huge and complex, so who runs it all? Surely, someone must be in charge? It's not the Internet service providers (ISPs) who connect you to the Internet, or the telecoms companies who supply phone lines and infrastructure. Nor is it national governments or the UN. The answer is that no single organization administers all websites and the content that flows between them.

Did you know?

Lurking beyond the Web that is accessible to search engines, lies the "deep web", millions of private pages and information held in databases, that search engines cannot reach.

Government interference

Search engines receive requests from national governments asking for the removal of material from their search results or, in Google's case, either from their search results or other Google products like YouTube or Google Groups. In the first six months of 2010, Google received more than 5,000 requests from the US government for material to be removed or information on users of Google products.

How big is the Web?

For a system that is all about information on any topic imaginable, from aardvarks to zip codes, it is surprising how little definitive data there is on the Web and its size. This is in part due to its constant growth and changing nature. A survey in January 2011 counted 273,301,445 websites. These generate more than 14 billion web pages.

Task force

The Internet Engineering Task Force (IETF) is an international, open community of network engineers, companies, and researchers who try to keep networks running smoothly whilst improving Internet standards.

W3C

Formed and led by Tim Berners-Lee, the World Wide Web Consortium (W3C) looks after the standards that underpin websites and web pages.

National restrictions

The World Wide Web's pioneers envisaged an open, free flow of information throughout the world, but national governments sometimes don't let that happen. Some websites that are accepted in one country may break the laws of another and are blocked or banned.

Many helpers

There may be no one in charge of the Web, but don't panic. Many organizations are involved in maintaining, managing, and planning different facets of the Internet. These include international working parties which ensure that web technology works in all languages, scripts, and cultures – an enormous task.

Internet Society

Formed in 1992, the Internet Society is a non-profit organization that has more than 44,000 members and tries to plan and campaign to avoid future problems with Internet growth.

Italy

Since 2006, gambling on foreign websites has been illegal in Italy. Gambling, betting, and bookmaking websites from abroad are blocked.

North Africa

During unrest in north Africa in 2011, the Twitter website was blocked in both Tunisia and Egypt to prevent it being used to organize protests.

> "The Internet is not a thing, a place, a single technology, or a mode of governance. It is an agreement."

John Gage, Director of Science, Sun Microsystems, Inc.

↗ Internet to splinternet?

The Internet has relied on agreement between many parties to survive and prosper worldwide. Could a lack of future agreement, censorship and other restrictions placed on websites by national governments lead to a "splinternet", with different standards in different nations? No one is certain, but changes are likely as more and more of the four billion people currently without access get online.

Walled gardens?

In the early days of the Web, major ISPs, like Compuserve and America OnLine (AOL), walled off their content, only allowing access to paying, registered users. After years of offering free content and services on the Web, many companies, including *The New York Times*, are returning to this model, and charging for access in an attempt to recoup the vast costs of their websites.

Net neutrality

There are other threats, besides government interference, that challenge the ability of the Internet to deliver all data equally to everyone – a principle known as network neutrality. Some ISPs and companies want to create a "fast lane" on the Internet, that can be used by customers who pay more for websites and data. Those who support neutrality fear that this would lead to an unequal and unfair service.

Political censorship

Some countries block websites that criticize the government or country, or give details of sensitive subjects such as anti-government protests and marches. In nations such as Cuba and Myanmar, with very low private Internet access, government-run cybercafés and access points may be heavily censored, with thousands of websites banned.

South Korea

South Koreans visiting websites with more than 100,000 members have to register with their real name and national identity card number.

Leaky bucket

Attempts to censor or remove material from the Internet are not always successful – it is sometimes described as a leaky bucket, because it is so easy to copy and redistribute information. Attempts at censorship can generate great international interest, and mirror sites that are copies of the original site often spring up, hosted in other countries.

Turkey

After its founder, Mustafa Kemal Atatürk was mocked in YouTube videos, Turkey banned the website in the country for two years.

Georgia

In 2008, during the war with Russia over the region of South Ossetia, the government of Georgia banned all websites that ended in .ru, originating from Russia.

The good side of the Web

The founders of the World Wide Web made it freely available because they saw it could be a powerful force for good. In many ways, they were right. In its relatively short life so far, the World Wide Web has been an astonishing success, helping to inform and transform millions of lives. It provides a platform for new businesses, puts people with shared interests in touch, and provides a convenient, regularly-updated source of news and entertainment for millions every day.

Free software

The Web holds a growing collection of computer programs that are free for anyone with Internet access to download. People often take these resources for granted, but it is quite astonishing that the results of thousands of hours of hard work are given away. The two main kinds of free software are freeware and open-source programs. Freeware is software that is free for personal or non-commercial use. Open-source programs go even further, offering the entire program code and background details so that fellow software designers can alter or improve the program.

Did you know?

OpenCourseWare offers free lecture notes, exam papers, and video tutorials on 2,000 different academic courses. More than a million students and educators visit the site each month.

Wayback Machine

Have you ever wanted to travel back in time? The Wayback Machine is a gigantic archive of web pages dating back to 1996. Users can see what a website's content was like at different points in the past – for free. In 2007, the California-based organization performed a massive web crawl in order to take a global snapshot of the World Wide Web. It catalogued and archived two billion web pages. Archives like this will be invaluable to future Internet historians.

Freecycle

In 2003, recycling activist Deron Beal sent out an email to about 40 friends and local charities around Tucson, Arizona, USA. He wanted to set up a scheme for people to offer unwanted goods to others for free rather than throw them away. The Freecycle Network now operates in more than 85 countries and has more than seven million members. Its online notice boards advertise all sorts of gifted items, from prams to printers.

Did you know?

Michelle Miles, a 19-year-old from Arkansas, USA, began a charitable cause on Facebook. Her "Race to End Cancer" has more than six million members and has raised more than £50,000 (US$80,000).

Sharing expertise

The Web is bursting with knowledge on a vast range of subjects. Experts and enthusiasts give up their time to offer insights and information on personal websites or take part in collaborative projects such as iFixit, which offers repair manuals for hundreds of electrical devices. Surfers can download sporting rules and coaching tips from governing bodies, identify wildlife they have spotted, learn a language, or get advice on how to improve their paintings, photography, or music, all for free.

Did you know?

On 10 December 2010, Freerice.com users donated more than 60 million grains of rice to starving people worldwide. All they had to do was click on advertisers' links on websites.

Helping others

Charities and campaign groups use the Web to raise awareness of issues. Their websites feature facts and figures, video case studies, and interviews. Many provide helpful free resources, such as advice on how to deal with bullying, eating disorders, alcohol, drugs, or gang violence. Charities can raise funds by running online campaigns or organizing virtual volunteering, where people donate their time or skills over the Internet to help a scheme some distance away.

The bad side of the Web

Most people build web pages in order to educate, inform, or entertain. Some, however, misuse the great resource at their fingertips, and play pranks, start rumours, or build websites full of lies. Some use the Web, email, and instant messaging to upset and intimidate people. Others spread malicious computer code that can damage computers or steal passwords, allowing criminals to divert money from victims' bank accounts.

Viruses and worms

Computer viruses are types of malware that make copies of themselves and run automatically on a computer, often destroying files or even erasing hard disks. When a file containing a virus is sent to another computer, that can become infected too. Worms are viruses that use network connections to spread automatically. Identified in 2008, the Conficker worm has infected millions of machines, including computers in the French Navy and British police. It may have caused more than £6 billion (US$9.5 billion) of damage.

Offensive sites

Many websites display images or discuss subjects, such as violence or sex, that are unsuitable for children and distasteful to many adults. Internet filters, such as Net Nanny, Safe Eyes, and Google's SafeSearch, can prevent these sites being viewed by people who do not want to or should not see them.

Did you know?

In 2009, 11 people were found guilty in China of using Trojans and other malware. They had stolen more than five million user names and passwords.

Malware

Computer software that is sent to your computer with mischievous or criminal intent is called malware. It includes viruses, worms, Trojans, and spyware. Malware can be just a harmless, if irritating, prank or designed for more serious purposes, such as stealing credit card and bank account details, or crippling a victim's computer. Malware is a massive problem, with around 60,000 new malware threats identified every day.

Phishing

Fake emails that seem to be from trusted sources, such as banks and Internet Service Providers, and that ask you to update or verify your personal details, are examples of phishing. What are they hoping to catch? People's banking and other personal details, which they can sell on to other criminals or use directly to make purchases.

Spam

In 2004, Bill Gates, founder of Microsoft, predicted that unsolicited bulk email (spam) would be stopped within 2 years. He was wrong. Despite the use of spam filters, junk emails still cram many people's inboxes. Most spam is sent out by zombies – PCs unknowingly infected with a virus or similar piece of malware that allows spammers to control them.

Trojans and backdoors

Trojan Horse programs act like legitimate software, such as a free game or virus scanner, to trick users into running them. Once installed, they can introduce further malware. Some Trojans install a backdoor – software that bypasses the computer's normal security to allow access to the entire machine. The US hacker Albert Gonzalez used backdoor programs to steal details for as many as 170 million ATM and credit cards. In 2010, he was sentenced to 20 years' imprisonment.

Did you know?

In 2010, the FBI finally captured Russian Oleg Nikolaenko, the "King of Spam". His infected computers were responsible for up to a third of the world's junk emails.

Cyber-bullying

Bullying is very upsetting both face-to-face and online. Cyber-bullying can involve a victim being ridiculed, harassed, unfairly excluded from a forum or online game, or repeatedly locked out of their social network accounts. Cyber-bullies may bombard their victim's phone or computer with threatening texts, emails, and instant messages, or send them spam and malware.

Fiction, not fact

Errors, pranks, and lies can spread, given credibility by appearing on a website. The dhmo.org website warns people of a dangerous liquid, dihydrogen monoxide. Seven million people have visited the site and calls for DHMO to be banned have been made by politicians in New Zealand and the USA – but DHMO is just another name for water!

Keeping us safe

Attempts at computer fraud and other crimes are an unpleasant fact of digital life. In their efforts to ward off attacks, police, software makers, and others involved with computer security give warnings of possible threats and come up with ways to keep computers and their users safe.

Be aware

The first and best line of defence against computer threats is to be a careful user. Keep antivirus software and other security patches up-to-date. You should also never open suspicious email attachments or reveal personal details online, and avoid counterfeit software and other illegal downloads.

Did you know?

In 2010, PandaLabs, the virus research network, estimated that 57,000 fake websites open every week. They mimic more famous sites, such as eBay, Amazon, and PayPal in an attempt to steal money.

Scams

Many scam websites or emails offer famous brands at low prices. People pay but never receive their goods. In 2009, London's e-crime unit closed down more than 1,200 fraudulent shopping sites. Fake charity sites, made to resemble real appeals, are another scam.

Password protection?

Hard-to-guess passwords offe[r] some protection. Unfortunatel[y] many people use the same we[b] password for all their accounts[.] Cyber-criminals can discover passwords with software that [go] through every possible charac[ter] combination. Longer passwor[ds] containing symbols and numb[ers] take longer to crack.

Top 10 weak passwords

1. password
2. 123456
3. qwerty
4. abc123
5. letmein
6. monkey
7. myspace1
8. password1
9. blink182
10. (your first name)

Fi...

A firew...
comm...
betwee...
Internet...
preferen...
through...
addresse...
preven...
gaining...
but it is...
software...

...mium

...asingly popular online business
...e, freemium websites offer basic
...a scaled-down version of their
...for free. The hope is that users will
...to upgrade to a premium, paid-for
...hat offers more content or features.
...by the Spotify music-streaming
...ype, and YouSendIt, for example.
...r model, some online games are
...ut charge for in-game items
..., such as weapons or skills.

Buyouts

Some companies offer such a strong
product or have so many visitors to their
website that bigger companies make a
takeover offer or buyout. There are even
websites that specialize in buying and
selling websites, such as Flippa. The
sums are usually small but occasionally
a big buyout occurs. In 2007, for
example, Yahoo! bought the Web
email company Zimbra for a cool
£220 million (US$350 million).

Did you know?

English schoolboy Tom
Hadfield started posting
football results in 1994 and
began Soccernet the
following year. In 1999, the
website sold for £25 million
(US$40 million).

...inner

...ashley Qualls started
...fering free graphics,
...on how to use them on
...aid £5 (US$8) for the domain
...verlife.com, but was soon
...hly cheques from advertisers
...4,000 (US$70,000). MySpace
...alls £1 million (US$1.5 million)
...choice of car for the site. She
...ed and, in 2009, relaunched it as a
...al networking site, WhateverLife 2.0.

Did you kno...

Malware atta...
literally out of...
2008, a lapto...
International...
was found...
the Gam...
which s...

Sites without ads

Some companies' websites are not
designed to turn a profit – they are
part of a company's marketing budget
and their job is simply to project a
positive image of the company.
Other websites raise money by selling
products directly, such as merchandise
or digital downloads. Some websites,
from small charities to Wikipedia, rely
on donations from individuals and
companies to cover their costs.

Antiv...
softw...

Antivirus pr...
for signs of...
check for fil...
the software...
of actions – ...
the file and...
Antivirus ma...
to existing...
threats, wh...

...dollar homepage

In 2005, UK student Alex Tew came
up with an ingenious way to pay for his
university education. He built a website
of one million pixels and sold off blocks
at 62p (US$1) per pixel to advertising
banners. The website was filled in
just 5 months and included a banner
advertising US actor Jack Black's rock
group Tenacious D and another
for *The Times* newspaper. The last
1,000 pixels were auctioned on eBay
for £23,800 (US$38,100)!

Did you know?

Fashion sales website Boo.com
went bust in 2000, having run up
costs of around £125 million
(US$200 million). Its spending
included flying a top hairdresser
from New York to London to style
the virtual hair of the website's
avatar, Miss Boo.

E-buying and selling

E-commerce is business performed using electronic systems. It's mostly buying and selling over the Internet or other computer networks and it has grown from a tiny pinprick of activity in the 1970s to a massive industry. In China alone in 2010, an estimated £210 billion (US$340 billion) changed hands in e-commerce transactions. And it's only going to get bigger and bigger...

craigslist

The online classified ads site, craigslist, is one of the most visited websites in the world, and receives **20 billion** page views every month.

1 million
• The number of new job listings each month on craigslist.

Every month **50 million** new adverts are placed on craigslist.

The cost to place an advert? Free!

BIG BUYS

eBay bought PayPal for **£930 million** (US$1.5 billion) in 2002. It has bought up more than 20 other companies including Skype and Shopping.com.

In 2009, Amazon paid **£750 million** (US$1,200 million) to buy clothing and shoe Internet store, Zappos.com. Amazon also owns Audible.com (audio entertainment), Pets.com, and IMDb.com (Internet Movie Database), among others.

amazon.com

Amazon, the world's largest online retailer, started out in the US in 1995 as an online bookstore, but now sells almost everything. In 2009, it enjoyed total sales of **£15.1 billion** (US$24.51 billion).

Amazon has **28,300 employees** worldwide.

SHOPPING FRENZY

On 15 December 2008, **6.3 million** items were ordered on Amazon. That's 72.9 every second.

ebay

Popular online auction site **eBay** started life as AuctionWeb created by Pierre Omidyar in California, USA, in 1995. The first item ever sold was a broken laser pointer that went for £10 (US$14.83).

eBay best-sellers (by frequency)

Every **3 seconds**: a woman's handbag
Every **9 seconds**: a CD
Every **21 seconds**: a mobile phone
Every **120 seconds**: a soccer shirt

90 million

eBay has around **90 million** users, spending more than **£35 billion** (US$57 billion) each year.

You can find anything on eBay...

In 2004, a **50,000-year-old mammoth** weighing 250,000 kg (550,000 lb) was sold for £61,000 (US$98,000).

A **stain on a floor of a garage** that looked a little like a portrait of Jesus Christ was sold on eBay for £950 (US$1,525.69).

In 2006, a **single Brussels sprout** left over from Christmas dinner fetched **£1,550** (US$2,490) in an eBay auction. The seller, Leigh Knight of Stockton, England, donated the money to Cancer Research.

Looking good
A piece of jewellery sells every **4 minutes** on eBay India, where it is the most popular category of items for sale.

In the USA **120,083,636** online shoppers averaged 24 online shopping sessions per year.

It's not just shopping!

Online banking is also taking off In 2009, the percentage of adult users in Europe's top five online banking nations were:

87%	Estonia
87%	Finland
82%	Netherlands
79%	Sweden
77%	Denmark

ONLINE OR IN STORE?

According to a US survey, in 2009–2010 the percentages of goods people bought online rather than in store were:

 74% electronics

 74% music and videos

 66% clothing

 61% books and magazines

 48% computer hardware and software

Did you know?

In 1994, PizzaNet (owned by Pizza Hut) became the first company to offer takeaway food over the Internet. The first order is thought to have been for a pepperoni and mushroom pizza with extra cheese.

Internet movie retailer **Netflix** ships out **1,000,000 DVDs** to customers every day.

Online shopping is huge in Japan. In 2010, **£140 billion** (US$185 billion) was spent by Japanese consumers

21% of people in the UK aged over 60 claim to do their weekly food shop online.

UK shoppers spent **£5.3 billion** (US$8.5 billion) online in November 2009.

Approximately **£72 billion** (US$115.6 billion) was spent on travel online in the USA in 2009.

iTunes

IN NUMBERS

10 billion
In February 2010, iTunes reached a music milestone when the total number of songs sold by the company reached 10 billion.

2,000,000
The number of Beatles songs sold on iTunes in their first week of release in November, 2010.

71
The age of the person who downloaded iTunes 10 billionth track *Guess Things Happen That Way*, by Johnny Cash. The man received a phone call from Apple's Steve Jobs and an iTunes gift card worth £6,200 (US$10,000).

7 billion
The number of apps (applications) downloaded from the iTunes store as of October, 2010.

WHAT DO YOU THINK?

Online consumers rely heavily on reviews. Here are the percentages of global consumers who would not buy certain products without first consulting reviews:

consumer electronics
40%

 a car
38%

 software
28%

 services
22%

 cosmetics
21%

淘宝网
Taobao.com

370 million
The number of Taobao users in 2010, when it was one of the top 15 most visited websites on the planet.

400 billion yuan
The value of transactions, equal to £38 billion (US$61 billion), on Taobao in 2010.

48,000
The number of items sold every minute in 2010 on China's leading e-commerce website, Taobao.

A world without wires

More than 100 years ago, radio waves were identified as a method of transmitting sound over long distances without wires to radio receivers. Wi-Fi is the name for technology that allows digital data to be transmitted using radio signals. Since the 1990s, the world has gone increasingly wireless to deliver mobile Internet connectivity to a massive range of machines, from tablet PCs to washing machines.

WiMAX aerials

WiMAX is Wi-Fi that uses powerful radio transmissions to enable signals carrying data to travel distances up to 50 km (30 miles) for fixed WiMAX stations, and 5–15 km (3–9 miles) for mobile stations. It gives moving vehicles broadband levels of Internet access.

Hotspots

A hotspot is an area of Wi-Fi coverage found in a public area such as a library, city centre, or even an International Space Station (below). Most are secured, requiring password access or payment to use the facility. Some are unsecured or deliberately free. You can also get small, portable routers called MiFi that generate a small, personal wireless hotspot allowing Wi-Fi use for phones and other personal devices.

Simple set-up

A simple home Wi-Fi set-up features a broadband Internet connection using a device called a wireless router. This receives data from the Internet and transmits it as a radio signal, usually up to a distance of 30–40 m (100–130 ft) indoors, and a little further outside.

Appliance science

Household products, from digital photo frames to fridges, are being fitted with Wi-Fi access as new applications are developed. A Wi-Fi-enabled fridge launched in 2011 can stream music into a kitchen, search for recipes online, and even order food from supermarkets.

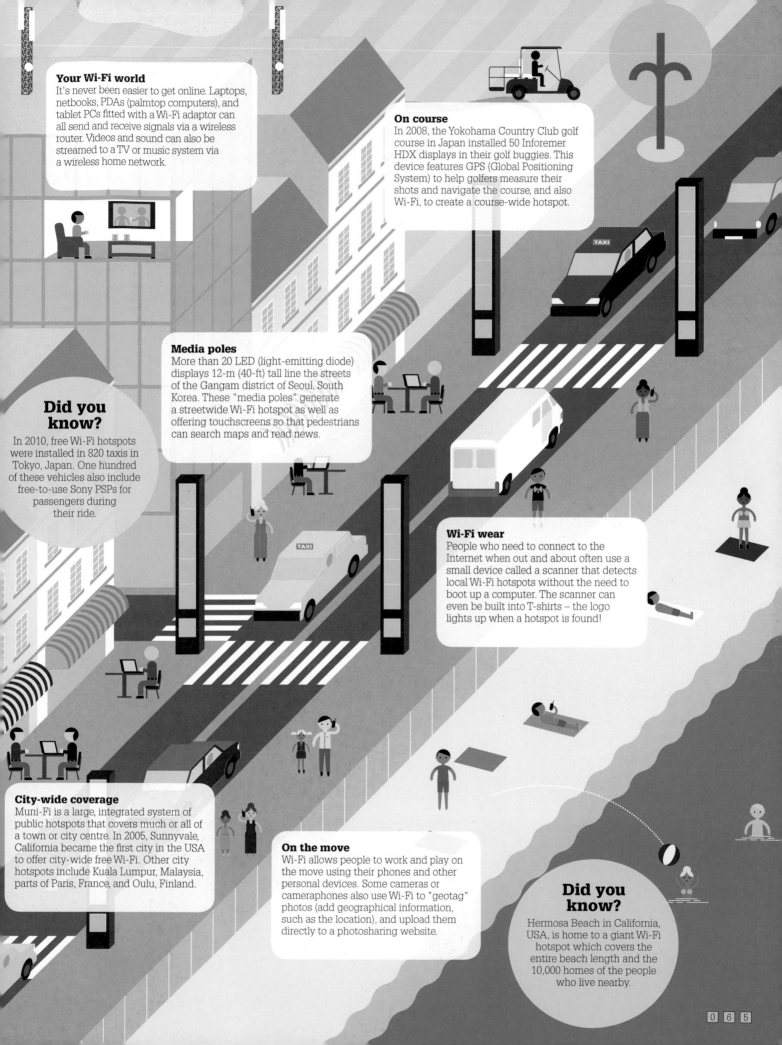

Your Wi-Fi world
It's never been easier to get online. Laptops, netbooks, PDAs (palmtop computers), and tablet PCs fitted with a Wi-Fi adaptor can all send and receive signals via a wireless router. Videos and sound can also be streamed to a TV or music system via a wireless home network.

On course
In 2008, the Yokohama Country Club golf course in Japan installed 50 Inforemer HDX displays in their golf buggies. This device features GPS (Global Positioning System) to help golfers measure their shots and navigate the course, and also Wi-Fi, to create a course-wide hotspot.

Media poles
More than 20 LED (light-emitting diode) displays 12-m (40-ft) tall line the streets of the Gangam district of Seoul, South Korea. These "media poles" generate a streetwide Wi-Fi hotspot as well as offering touchscreens so that pedestrians can search maps and read news.

Did you know?
In 2010, free Wi-Fi hotspots were installed in 820 taxis in Tokyo, Japan. One hundred of these vehicles also include free-to-use Sony PSPs for passengers during their ride.

Wi-Fi wear
People who need to connect to the Internet when out and about often use a small device called a scanner that detects local Wi-Fi hotspots without the need to boot up a computer. The scanner can even be built into T-shirts – the logo lights up when a hotspot is found!

City-wide coverage
Muni-Fi is a large, integrated system of public hotspots that covers much or all of a town or city centre. In 2005, Sunnyvale, California became the first city in the USA to offer city-wide free Wi-Fi. Other city hotspots include Kuala Lumpur, Malaysia, parts of Paris, France, and Oulu, Finland.

On the move
Wi-Fi allows people to work and play on the move using their phones and other personal devices. Some cameras or cameraphones also use Wi-Fi to "geotag" photos (add geographical information, such as the location), and upload them directly to a photosharing website.

Did you know?
Hermosa Beach in California, USA, is home to a giant Wi-Fi hotspot which covers the entire beach length and the 10,000 homes of the people who live nearby.

Smartphone

Mobile phones have become so sophisticated some are essentially pocket-sized computers. These "smartphones" feature a fully-fledged operating system such as iOS, Android, or Symbian, can run thousands of different small programs known as apps, and boast more processing power than many 10-year-old PCs.

iPhone

Apple's fourth generation smartphone was launched in 2010. Containing 16 or 32GB of storage, the phone's steel and glass casing measures 11.52 x 5.86 cm (4.5 x 2.30 in) and is just 0.93 cm (0.37 in) thick. Central to smartphones' success is the vast range of apps available. According to Apple more than 300,000 different apps, from games to business software, now exist for iPhones.

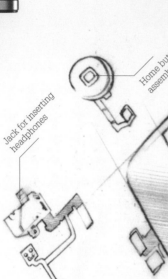

Home button assembly

Jack for inserting headphones

Lower antenna and speaker

30-pin socket connector

Power button and sensor cable

Motor to allow vibration

Plastic frame to protect glass

1 Microphone
The iPhone has twin microphones; the main one at the bottom of the phone is used for calls and voice-controlled apps, and a second microphone at the top helps to cancel out background noise and make music and calls clearer.

2 Screen
The 8.9-cm (3.5-in.) liquid crystal display (LCD) is one of the highest resolution screens around. This allows the device to display ultra-sharp text and graphics. The screen is protected by a layer of glass chemically treated to be 20 times stiffer and 30 times harder than plastic.

3 A4 Chip
The iPhone's main processor is a complete system on a chip. It has a lot of work to do – from handling the phone's graphics and running multiple apps at the same time, to interpreting touch gestures on its screen and displaying video in real time.

4 Camera
There are two cameras featured on the iPhone 4. The rear camera has 5 megapixel resolution and can be used for capturing both still images and video. The camera on the front of the phone is for use with Apple's video-calling app, FaceTime.

5 Lithium-ion battery
A 1420mAh powerpack inside the iPhone is rechargeable and gives up to 6 hours of call time, 10 hours of WiFi use to send messages or surf the Internet, and up to 40 hours of audio playback to listen to music, podcasts, or audiobooks.

"Today Apple is going to reinvent the phone."
Steve Jobs, 2007

Steve Jobs is the CEO and co-founder of Apple computer.

How a touchscreen works

Selection
The latest smartphone screens are touch sensitive. The user swipes across the screen to find the app they want to use, which they open by touching the appropriate icon.

Touch registered
A grid of sensors below the screen registers the touch as electrical signals. They detect where the touch occurred, and the data is sent as electrical impulses to the processor.

Gesture recognized
The processor interprets the touch gesture made, matching it to those held in its memory and also checking what that gesture means in any specific app being run at the time.

Action completed
The gesture has been recognized and the action of launching the app is performed by the phone's processor. This all happens smoothly and in an instant.

Vibration button

Volume up and down buttons

Steel outer frame acts as antenna

512 megabytes of memory

WiFi antenna

Micro-SIM card holder

Front facing VGA camera

Li-ion

Plastic frame to house components

Back sheet of ultra durable glass

2

3

4

5

Text talk

Everyone may be talking about the latest technology – multi-touch, multimedia devices, video calls, and photo messaging – but Internet communication is still dominated by messages typed out in text form. Billions of emails, text messages, and instant messages are sent every day, and many millions of people update their blogs.

Sent (286 messages)

 Get mail | **Delete** **Junk** | **Reply** **Reply all** **Forward** | **New message** | **Note** **To do**

Mailboxes

▶ Inbox

 You've got mail
A report in 2009 estimated that there were **1.4 billion** email users that year. This is expected to rise to **1.9 billion** by 2013.

30

The average size of a typical email is 30 kilobytes (KB).

The number of worldwide email accounts is projected to increase from more than **2.9 billion** in 2010, to more than **3.8 billion** by 2014.

Subject: Email

Email users by region in 2010:

North America **14%**

Europe **23%**

Asia/Pacific **47%**

Rest of the world **16%**

Watch your words
In a 2008 report, **32%** of people admitted to sending an angry or embarrassing email to the wrong person by accident.

 **Check first**
In 2006, a member of staff at the University of California, Berkeley law school, USA, was writing an email when he pressed **"Reply all"** by mistake. He sent emails of congratulation not only to the **800** students who had received a place at the university, but to all **7,000** students who had applied. He had to send out many further emails of apology.

4 million

The number of spam emails sent to Bill Gates during 2004. Nearly all of these were filtered out by anti-spam software.

 An average of **247 billion** emails were sent each day in 2009.

  In the time it takes you to read this sentence, around **20 million** emails have been sent.

Business or pleasure?
In 2010, **75%** of all email accounts belonged to private consumers, and **25%** to business users.

Too much spam

In 2009, a security report estimated that **85.8%** of all emails were spam – unrequested and unwanted junk emails that are sent out in bulk to vast numbers of email addresses, filling inboxes and wasting time as users delete them.

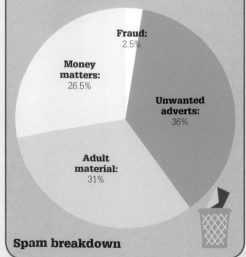

Fraud: **2.5%**

Money matters: **26.5%**

Unwanted adverts: **36%**

Adult material: **31%**

Spam breakdown

Blogs

Starting out as diaries or journals displayed online, blogs get their name from "web log" (journal), a term invented by American blogger Jorn Barger in 1997. Blogs consist of posts or entries, that are mostly text but can contain images, videos, or links, with the latest posting displayed first.

One in five bloggers update their blogs daily, and more than half operate **two or more blogs**.

Around **60%** of bloggers are between the ages of 18 and 44, and more than **70%** are male.

49% The percentage of total bloggers worldwide that are from the US.

In numbers

133,000,000
The number of different blogs listed on leading blog directory Technorati since 2002.

77% The percentage of Internet users who read blogs.

15% An estimated 15% of bloggers spend **ten hours** a week blogging.

1901 The year the world's oldest blogger, Bernando Lapello, was born. The Brazilian is the author of the *Age Less Live More* blog.

200 million
To date, the world's most popular blogger is Chinese writer and rally car driver Han Han, whose blog attracts more than 200 million visitors.

Text messaging and IM

The short-message service (SMS) featured on mobile phones allows text messages up to 160 characters long to be sent to other mobile users. Texting is big business with millions signing up to text alert services to get the latest news or sports scores delivered by text.

The first SMS text ever, sent by engineer Neil Papworth to Vodafone's Richard Jarvis on 3 December 1992, read "Merry Christmas".

There are an estimated **3.6 billion** global users of SMS worldwide.

A staggering **6.1 trillion** SMS messages were sent in 2010, that's almost 200,000 every second.

According to a study in 2009, 95% of all SMS messages are read within 4–15 minutes and replied to within the hour.

An average of **11 million** SMS text messages were sent in the UK every hour during 2009. In the same year, just two countries, the United States and the Philippines, were responsible for 35% of all SMS sent.

In 2010, two British 23-year-old climbers trapped 3,500 m (11,500 ft) up western Europe's highest mountain, Mount Blanc, on the border of France and Italy, were rescued after sending an SMS for help to a friend back in England, who then called the rescue services.

An SMS message uses **140 bytes** of memory – a typical single mp3 song uses the same amount of memory as 4,000 SMS messages.

Instant messaging (IM) programs are another popular method of communicating between two people using computers. AOL Instant Messenger (AIM) is used by **15.4 million** people each month. On average, users spend 43 minutes on AIM each day.

In 2009, some **40 million** users logged in at the same time during peak hours on Windows Live Messenger, where users can perform instant messaging to each other.

Send

TxtMsgs

The 160 character limit for text messages has seen a whole texting language build up full of unusual abbreviations to save space.

LOL	laugh out loud
BTW	by the way
ROFL	rolling on floor laughing
a2m1	*A demain* – French for "see you tomorrow"
nph	*no puedo hablar* – Spanish for "I can't talk now"
GuK	*Gruß und Kuss* – German for "love and kisses"

Eye in the sky

Fifteen years ago, people would have thought you mad if you suggested using a PC to fly round a virtual Earth, zooming out to see whole continents, then zooming in to see your own home. Yet, through speedier Internet access, better computers, and smart programming, a range of mapping services allows you to do just that. The Italian city of Rome, for example, can be explored in many different ways.

Bird's-eye view
From a distant aerial view of a city or region, many mapping programs allow you to zoom in closer and closer. This clear, bird's-eye view gives an interesting perspective on St Peter's Basilica, inside the Vatican City.

Road maps
There are a number of detailed street and road map services available for free on the Web. Users can plot routes between different points, zoom in close for individual street directions, and bookmark locations for later use.

The night sky
Some mapping programs and web apps turn the focus away from Earth. They observe stars, planets, comets, and other phenomena in the night sky, and plot how these shift during a year. Many of these astronomy apps are free.

Gathering data

Collecting all the imagery for a complete, detailed visual map of all parts of the world is a daunting task. A range of different techniques is used to image the Earth in both close up and from long distance.

On the ground
Google's fleet of street cars, trikes, and snowmobiles generate ground-level imagery for use with Google Street View. Fitted 2.5 m (8 ft) above the ground on each vehicle's mast are nine cameras that together generate 360-degree views.

Sharing resources
On some apps, users upload and share their own photos, tagged to locations. This image of Rome's Pantheon is from Panoramio. Within two years of its launch, Panoramio boasted more than five million user-submitted images.

In the air
Many mapping and virtual world projects use aerial photography taken from low-level aircraft. Photography for bird's-eye-view maps is usually taken from a 45-degree angle to the ground. This helps give a simple, 3-D-like perspective.

The view on the street
Rome's Trevi Fountain can be seen from ground level using Street layers on Bing Maps and Google Earth. These display panoramic photos along various streets in the world but are controversial because of privacy issues.

Up in space
Landsat satellites have been orbiting our planet since 1972, beaming back thousands of visible-light and infrared images of Earth's surface. These have been used by scientists, environmentalists, and governments, as well as by recent online mapping services.

Weather view
Satellite weather images were among the first large-scale maps available on the Internet. Data from weather satellites is now incorporated into some mapping programs, so they display clouds over the world in real-time.

Reconstructions in 3-D
Using freely-available software, Web users can build and display 3-D models of buildings, such as this reconstruction of the ruins of the Colosseum. Google has even modelled different tree species and "planted" them across Google Earth.

Opera House, Sydney, Australia →
This 3-D image shows the unusual concrete shells that form the distinctive roofs of the Opera House in Sydney Harbour.

← Manhattan, New York City, USA
This bird's-eye view shows the famous grid system of Manhattan, one of five boroughs in New York City. It is the most populated of all the boroughs.

Tsunami destruction, Indonesia →
You can also see changing landscapes. These images show an area of Indonesia before (right) and after (far right) the tsunamis (giant waves) of 2004.

← Wilkins Ice Shelf, Antarctica
This ice shelf about 150 km (93 miles) long is breaking up and floating away from the Antarctic mainland. An overhead view shows the large chunks of ice that have already broken off.

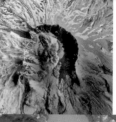

← Mount St Helens, Washington, USA
Hover above the large crater of Mount St Helens, an active volcano that still spouts ash and steam. In 1980, it erupted violently, killing 57 people.

← Mount Fuji, Japan
Soar over the snow-covered cone of Japan's highest mountain and one of the country's most famous landmarks. Mount Fuji is a dormant volcano that last erupted in 1708.

↑ Matterhorn, Italy and Switzerland
At 4,478 m (14,692 ft), the Matterhorn is one of the highest peaks in the Alps. Shaped like a pyramid, it towers over the border between Italy and Switzerland.

← Three Gorges Dam, Hubei Province, China
The largest hydroelectrical dam in the world, the Three Gorges Dam can be spotted spanning the Yangtze River. China hopes it will reduce reliance on coal power and help reduce flooding along the river.

← Hong Kong, China
Zoom in and look closer at the 3-D skyscrapers of Hong Kong, one of the world's top financial centres. The city's tallest building is the International Commerce Centre at 484 m (1,588 ft).

Where do you want to go?

↑ Bird's Nest, Beijing, China
This spectacular stadium made of steel beams was the centre of the 2008 Olympic Games. You can look inside the stadium and see activity inside.

Using software available on the Web, you can explore a virtual Earth that has been put together using images from satellites, aerial photography, and other sources. Travel the planet – below the oceans, flying over its highest peaks, and even beyond – Earth's natural wonders are all there to see along with world-famous cities and landmarks.

← Grasberg mine, New Guinea, Indonesia
Grasberg is the world's largest gold mine and third-largest copper mine. This overhead view, and the buildings around the site, give some idea of its scale.

Boneyard, Tuscon, Arizona, USA →
More than 4,000 retired US military aircraft can be seen lined up in the Arizona desert. The dry climate prevents the aircraft from deteriorating quickly.

↑ Wreck of the *Titanic*, Atlantic Ocean
An undersea, 3-D view allows exploration of shipwrecks. The *Titanic*, a liner that hit an iceberg, sank, and split in two in 1912, is one of the most famous wrecks.

Mangroves, Bangladesh →
From high in the sky you can see channels of the River Ganges snake towards the Indian Ocean. This is a huge area of mangrove forest called the Sunderbans.

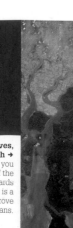

← **Venice, Italy**
The city of Venice stands on 117 small islands on a marshy lagoon. Instead of roads, there is a system of canals navigated by boats with paths for pedestrians.

← **Uluru, Australia**
This sandstone rock is a sacred site to aboriginal Australians. It looms out of the desert and glows red and orange in the sunlight.

ake Titicaca, u and Bolivia
n in the Andes ntains, at an ude of 3,811 m 500 ft), Lake Titicaca e largest lake in h America.

← **Easter Island (Rapa Nui), South Pacific**
Explore Easter Island and find the enormous *mo'ai*, statues built by the Rapa Nui people between the 10th and 17th centuries CE, that stare out to sea.

→ **Hippos, Tanzania**
Some views reveal wildlife in the landscape. Images from a low-flying plane show a large herd of hippos swimming in a river in Tanzania.

6°53'53.28"S 31°11'14.78"E

al Sea, Kazakhstan and Uzbekistan →
he rivers that fed the huge Aral Sea were diverted for irrigation 1960s. Images w the lake has shrunk volume between 1989) and 1999 (far right).

↑ **The Pentagon, Virginia, USA**
The headquarters of the US Department of Defense looks impressive from the air. The five-sided structure is the world's largest office building by floor area.

← **Andromeda**
The nearest galaxy to ours is Andromeda, 2.5 million light-years away. It is a spiral galaxy and contains twice as many stars as the Milky Way.

← **Eiffel Tower, Paris, France**
This 3-D view of the Eiffel Tower in Paris shows how the structure dominates the city's skyline. It's the second-largest building in France and was built in 1889.

↓ **Crab Nebula**
Look deep into our galaxy, the Milky Way, and you will find the Crab Nebula, the remains of a star that exploded in the year 1054.

← **Mariana Trench, Pacific Ocean**
You can even dive below the surface of the sea and explore the deepest point on Earth, the Mariana Trench at a depth of 11,000 m (36,000 ft).

Great Barrier ef, Australia
e world's largest f system can be en from outer space. stretches more than 00 km (1,600 miles) d teems with a verse range of life.

← **Nile Delta, Egypt**
From the air, you can see the River Nile cutting through the vast empty expanse of the Sahara Desert. Fertile green areas line its banks and mark its delta as it reaches the Mediterranean Sea (top).

← **Bosphorus, Turkey**
The Bosphorus Strait is the border between Europe (far left) and Asia (left). Two bridges span the strait, below the centre of the image. The strait flows between the Black Sea (top) and the Sea of Marmara (below).

↑ **Santorini, Greece**
Several volcanic islands make up Santorini in the Aegean Sea. A huge volcanic eruption around 3,500 years ago left a huge, sea-filled depression in the centre of the islands.

Olympus Mons, Mars →
On Mars lies a giant volcano that rises 24 km (15 miles) above the planet's surface. Olympus Mons is the highest mountain in the Solar System.

↑ **Mars**
Head further out into the Solar System and explore the rusty-red surface of Mars. Tens of thousands of craters mark its surface, created by rocky asteroids that crashed into the planet.

t Plains, estern USA
this huge expanse d has been used ng or grazing k. Where the land ater is brought in e the land.

Moon →
There are many ways to explore the Moon online. You can zoom into its surface, tour the Apollo spacecraft landing sites, and see 3-D models of some of the craft.

← **Lambert Crater, Moon**
Lambert is one of millions of craters on the Moon, many of which have been named. Craters can be up to many hundreds of kilometres wide.

What's a wiki?

Wikipedia

The biggest, most famous wiki of all is the online encyclopedia Wikipedia. It is a collection of wikis in different languages, over 260 in total, with the biggest in the English language containing more than 3.5 million articles and all available on the Web for free.

A wiki is a part of a website that is open so that lots of different people can contribute to and edit its content. Users can access and edit the page online using their regular web browser. Wikis can be useful in lots of ways, such as when a group of people from different countries want to work together to produce a single letter or article about a subject. Wiki pages can be easily and quickly updated and usually feature links to other web pages.

Wales and Sanger

As the new century began, Americans Larry Sanger and Jimmy Wales were involved in building an online encyclopedia called Nupedia. Sanger learnt about wikis from a contributor to WikiWikiWeb and convinced Wales and others to try it out. Wikipedia launched in 2001 with 20,000 articles created by the end of that first year.

The first wiki

Ward Cunningham, an American software developer, began work on the first wiki in 1994. He created an open, editable set of web pages to help programmers and other computer technicians share ideas more efficiently. He added this to his own company's website in 1995.

Not for profit

Wikipedia is one of the world's top ten most visited websites. If run for profit, advertising on its pages would generate hundreds of millions of dollars. But its founders have resisted turning it into a business, instead relying on fundraising and donations from individuals and organizations. Both Google and the charity set up by eBay founder, Pierre Omidyar, recently made million-dollar donations.

Wikileaks

The most controversial of all wikis is the Wikileaks site launched in 2006. It contains private, secret, and classified documents on military, business, and governments – leaked to the site usually by anonymous sources. Wikileaks is now banned in a number of countries.

Other wikis

Wikis exist for all sorts of subjects including music lyrics (Lyricwiki), medicine (Ask DrWiki), Wikitravel, and *World of Warcraft* (Wowpedia). One of the largest wikis is Hudong, an enormous Chinese online encyclopedia using the wiki format, which contains more than three million articles.

Quick, quick

Cunningham named his first open editable website WikiWikiWeb after the free shuttle bus that runs from Honolulu airport, Hawaii. WikiWiki means "quick, quick" in Hawaiian.

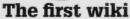

Checking sources

Wikipedia can be a tremendous resource but, due to errors and pranks, it is recommended that other sources are used to double check facts. When French composer Maurice Jarre died in 2009, many newspaper articles included a quote from him. However the quote had been made up and added to Wikipedia by Irish student Shane Fitzgerald.

"Imagine a world in which every single person on the planet is given free access to the sum of all human knowledge. That's what we're doing."

Jimmy Wales

Edit wars

Sometimes, topics elicit strong opinions. An edit war occurs when rival editors keep changing an article to fit it in with their view. Many edit wars are trivial, but some are serious. The Wikipedia entry on the Iraq War, for instance, went through more than 12,000 different edited versions.

WikiCriticism

Critics point out that some Wikipedia articles are poorly written or produced by non-experts on complex topics, so may contain poorly-explained facts or mistakes. Sometimes people vandalize articles, present opinions as facts, or add straight lies, such as in 2006 when English soccer player David Beckham was defined as an 18th-century Chinese goalkeeper.

Error-ridden?

In 2005, the scientific journal *Nature* conducted a study comparing 42 science articles in Wikipedia with the online version of *Encyclopaedia Britannica*. The survey revealed that *Britannica* had 123 errors while Wikipedia had 162, an average of 3.9 per article.

The millionth entry

In March 2006, an entry on Jordanhill railway station in Scotland became the English edition of Wikipedia's one millionth article. Within three and a half years, a further two million articles were added on every conceivable topic from aardvarks to zippers including the smell of new cars, wife-carrying competitions, and National Towel Day!

How editing works

Behind Wikipedia lies a tiny number of paid staff but an enormous community of many thousands of people who give up their leisure time to write and debate new articles, and repair or update existing articles.

⊙ At the top of every page on Wikipedia is an edit button. Clicking on this calls up the page in editable form complete with codes for formatting the text and adding tables, links, and images.

⊙ Wikipedia has online help guides and a sandbox, where people can experiment. Material in the sandbox is erased automatically every 12 hours. The history tab also shows earlier versions of an article.

⊙ Any edited page can be previewed and saved. Other editors may debate the new article or make comments on that article's separate talk page.

The age of the Internet

The Internet developed slowly and organically, as computer and telecoms experts pieced together the necessary new technology and software to enable computers of different types to "talk" to each other and form networks. Today, the pace of change on the Internet is incredibly fast. A strong, well planned website or Internet application can become a global success in just a few months – or even weeks.

1978
In the US, Gary Thuerk sends the first spam email, advertising DEC computer systems. More than 900 users receive the email and are not amused.

↓ 1992
The world's first smartphone, IBM's Simon, is demonstrated and goes on sale to the public the following year. It boasts a touchscreen, calendar, and email features.

1969
ARPA's computer network ARPANET begins with four locations, called nodes: at the University of Utah, two Californian universities, and the Stanford Research Institute. A five-letter message was successfully sent an hour later.

↓ 1974
In *A Protocol for Packet Network Interconnection*, Vinton Cerf and Bob Kahn explain the software (now developed as TCP/IP) that would allow different computers and networks to communicate with each other to form an "inter-network".

↓ 1988
In the US, student Robert Tappan Morris writes the Morris worm, one of the first major computer security attacks, which disrupts parts of the Internet. Morris receives a 3-year suspended sentence and a fine of £6,250 (US$10,000).

↓ 1982
The smiley emoticon ":-)" is proposed by US computer scientist Scott Fahlman on Carnegie Mellon University's bulletin boards.

↓ 1957
The Soviet Union launches the first satellite, *Sputnik*. In response, the USA sets up the Advanced Research Projects Agency (ARPA) to fund research into technology.

1988
In Finland, Jarkko Oikarinen launches the multi-user chat program IRC (Internet Relay Chat), a forerunner of online instant messaging.

1990
The first search engine, called Archie, is created by Alan Emtage, a student at McGill University in Montreal, Quebec, Canada.

1993
The Mosaic web browser is released. It is credited with popularizing early use of the World Wide Web.

1967
The UK's National Physical Laboratory develops packet switching – a way of sending data over a network by breaking it up into small units, or packets.

1979
The online discussion board Usenet launches. It allows people to send posts to different newsgroups, divided into topics.

↓ 1989
Sir Tim Berners-Lee begins work on the World Wide Web while working at CERN, Switzerland.

↑ 1971
US computer programmer Ray Tomlinson starts the first email system on ARPANET. He uses the "@" symbol to identify unique users and sends the first email message.

1977
US businessmen Dennis Hayes and Dale Heatherington develop the personal computer modem (a device to connect to the Internet) and sell it to computer hobbyists.

1984
The domain name system is introduced, making addresses on the Internet more informative and easier to remember.

↑ 1991
In the UK, the first webcam is set up in Cambridge University's computer lab. It films a coffee machine so that researchers can see if the pot is empty or not without leaving their seats. The webcam stays switched on until 2001.

In February 2005, three former PayPal workers – Chad Hurley, Steve Chen, and Jawed Karim – started to build a video website. The very first clip uploaded in April (and still on the site) shows Karim at San Diego Zoo, California. YouTube launched in November 2005. By July 2006, 65,000 new videos were being added every day. Less than a year after its launch, YouTube was sold to Google.

"I'd like to know what the Internet is going to look like in 2050. Thinking about it makes me wish I were 8 years old."

Vinton Cerf, 2008, US computer scientist and Internet pioneer

1994
Telecoms company AT&T pay for the first web banner advert. It appears on *Wired* magazine's *HotWired* web magazine.

1996
HoTMaiL, the first web-based email service, goes live.

← 2000
The dot-com bubble bursts and many Internet businesses go bankrupt. In the next 18 months, around £3 trillion (US$5 trillion) is wiped off the value of technology firms.

2006
Google buys YouTube for £1 billion (US$1.65 billion).

2008
eBay retailer Jack Sheng becomes the first person to earn a customer feedback rating of one million. Sheng started his gadgets business with just £300 (US$500) and has built a £25-million (US$40-million) empire.

1994
The launch of whitehouse.gov gives the President of the United States an online presence.

↓ 1996
Adobe launches its Flash Player, adding animation, video and audio to web pages.

Adobe

↓ 2000
Google's index hits the milestone of one trillion unique URLs (web addresses).

1,000,000,000,000

↑ 2004
The Mozilla Foundation releases the first version of its Firefox web browser.

twitter

↑ 2006
American entrepreneur Jack Dorsey launches a trial of Twitter and publishes the first tweet: "just setting up my twttr".

2008
Hulu launches in the USA. The service streams TV shows and movies. By October 2008, it has 30 million users and has streamed more than 260 million pieces of content.

1998
Google launches, boasting an index of 25 million pages and a clean, uncluttered user interface.

2001
Jimmy Wales launches Wikipedia, the popular online encyclopedia created by volunteers.

2004
The photo-sharing website Flickr is born, as digital photography increases in popularity.

2006
Social networking site Facebook, originally just for Harvard students, is made available to everyone.

amazon

↑ 1995
Online retailer Amazon.com launches. The company does not make a profit until 2001.

napster

↑ 1999
In the USA, 18-year-old Shawn Fanning launches Napster, a peer-to-peer (P2P) file-sharing service. It attracts both large numbers of users and criticism and legal action from the music industry.

↑ 2003
Apple launches the iTunes store, selling 250,000 songs within 24 hours. Eight years later, more than 10 billion songs have been downloaded.

2007
In the UK, the BBC launches its multimedia streaming service, iPlayer, on Christmas Day. By October 2010, it is serving 139 million pieces of radio, TV, or film content every month.

↑ 1995
Microsoft Internet Explorer launches as an add-on pack to the Windows 95 operating system.

1997
The web address **business.com** sells for £80,000 (US$150,000).

2003
Internet voice-over service Skype launches.

YouTube™

↑ 2005
Video-sharing website YouTube launches. By July the following year, there are up to 100 million video views each day.

↗ 2010
The file-sharing site the Pirate Bay (opened in 2003) is shut down, after legal battles with the Recording Industry Association of America (RIAA) and Motion Picture Association of America (MPAA).

↑ Robot helper
Preserving past media for the future in digital form is a massive job. The Qidenus robotic digitizer turns and scans book pages with perfect accuracy. It can scan an amazing 2,500 pages per hour with no human intervention.

Digitizing hard copy

Not long ago, hard copy was king. Everything was written down, typed, printed, photocopied, or filed on paper. Then came the rise of computing and the Internet. These days, most new documents and many books are created in electronic form. At the same time, older materials are being scanned to create digital versions that can be kept on computers. Digital files can be stored in their millions and sent over the Internet in seconds.

↑ In the library
Libraries of the past held vast quantities of books, newspapers, and journals. Today, many libraries are restricting their physical collections in order to give space to PCs or terminals that offer Internet access.

← E-readers
Weighing less than one printed book, an e-reader can hold up to 5,000 books in electronic form. It offers on-the-go portability as well as time-saving features, such as fast keyword searches through millions of words.

The shift to digital media

Magazines, photos, books, and CDs are all physical media – unlike digital files, they take up masses of space, take time to be delivered after ordering, are difficult to update, and can be bulky to carry. For these reasons, there has been a huge shift from physical to digital media that can be stored on electronic systems.

→ MP3 player
Portable digital music players are memory chips or mini hard drives linked to a small sound card and an amplifier. This 16 GB iPod nano, launched in 2010, holds 4,000 tracks and weighs a mere 21 g (0.75 oz).

Music media

After decades of vinyl records, compact discs (CDs) arrived in the 1980s. The big shift to digital media, though, came with the ability to copy individual CD tracks into digital formats, such as MP3, WAV, or FLAC files. At last music was easy to store, play, and share over the Internet. Today, billions of tracks are downloaded from pay sites, such as iTunes and Amazon.

← Record store
A large record store held thousands of LPs – dinner-plate-sized vinyl discs that featured 20 to 40 minutes of music per side. Today, music stores mostly sell CDs, but tracks are increasingly bought online instead.

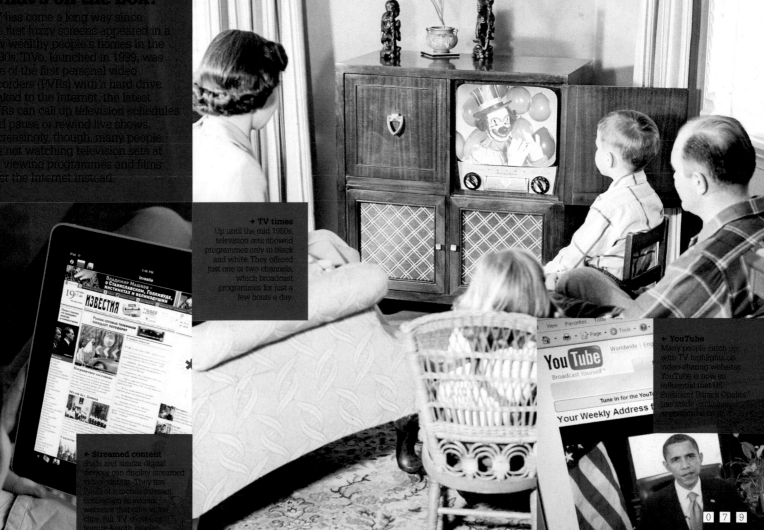

What's on the box?

TV has come a long way since the first fuzzy screens appeared in a few wealthy people's homes in the 1930s. TiVo, launched in 1999, was one of the first personal video recorders (PVRs) with a hard drive. Linked to the Internet, the latest PVRs can call up television schedules and pause or rewind live shows. Increasingly, though, many people are not watching television sets at all, viewing programmes and films over the Internet instead.

→ TV times
Up until the mid 1950s, television sets showed programmes only in black and white. They offered just one or two channels, which broadcast programmes for just a few hours a day.

← Streamed content
iPads and similar digital devices can display streamed video content. They use Wi-Fi or a mobile Internet connection to access websites that offer video clips, full TV shows, or feature-length movies.

← YouTube
Many people catch up with TV highlights on video-sharing websites. YouTube is now so influential that US President Barack Obama has made online video appearances on it.

E-reader

E-books are books in a digital format, such as a wordprocessing document or a PDF (portable document file), that can be read on a computer, tablet, or smartphone. E-readers are devices devoted to storing and displaying e-books and other text documents. They allow students, travellers, and commuters to carry large numbers of books, newspapers, PDFs, and other documents in one small package.

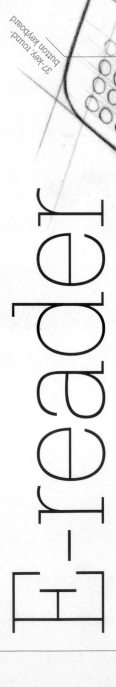

E-ink pearl display

37-key round-button keyboard

Four-direction cursor controller

Internal support structure

E-ink controller chip

190 mm x 123 mm   **8.5 mm**
(7.5 in x 4.8 in)   (0.3 in) thick

Amazon Kindle

Amazon's third generation Kindle was launched in 2010. At 247 g (9 oz), it weighs less than most paperbacks, yet its 4 GB of memory can hold an astonishing 3,500 books. The device can synchronize with Amazon's Kindle store, allowing users to browse the opening chapters of hundreds of thousands of books, buy books electronically, and download them straight onto the device.

1 Keyboard

Users can type in a word to look up its meaning in the Kindle's built-in dictionary. Annotations can also be typed into a book, which are stored in the memory. The Alt key allows certain shortcuts and also launches a surprise *Minesweeper* game to play.

2 Speakers

The Kindle's two small speakers can output mp3 sound files, such as music or audiobooks. In addition, an experimental feature on the device can convert the text of a book into speech to read a book aloud.

3 Battery

A 1750mAh lithium polymer battery takes up much of the space inside the Kindle case. Due to the very low power demands of the e-ink screen, and with no hard disk to keep spinning, the battery can last up to 4 weeks between charges.

4 Micro-USB port

Books and documents can be moved to the Kindle from a computer via the micro-USB port, which doubles as the way in which the Kindle's battery is charged in around 4.5 hours.

5 Logic board

The Kindle's logic board (printed circuit board) contains 4 GB of memory, an e-ink controller chip built by Epson, and a multimedia processor. There is also a chip devoted to managing the unit's power and a Wolfson stereo codec chip to help power the Kindle's twin speakers.

6 Wi-Fi card

An Atheros AR6102G 802.11bg chip allows books, newspapers, and other documents to be delivered wirelessly to the Kindle using Amazon's Whispernet data service. A typical book takes under a minute to load onto the machine.

Graphite outer casing

"The vision is that you should be able to get any book – not just any book in print, but any book that's ever been in print – on this device."
Jeff Bezos, 2007

Jeff Bezos founded Amazon in 1994 to sell books over the Internet. It has grown to become America's largest online retailer and, in 2007, released its first Kindle e-reader.

E-ink

Unlike laptop and smartphone screens, an e-ink display doesn't fade or wash out in bright sunlight and is easy on the eyes when reading. The display is a plastic film coated with millions of tiny microcapsules. Each capsule contains positively-charged white particles and negatively-charged black particles. When a grid of electrodes below the film activates, signals in the grid attract one type of particle and repel the other. The repelled particles move to the top of the capsule, where they are visible to the human eye.

White particles attracted to grid

Black particles repelled to top

White particles repelled to top

E-ink capsule full of clear fluid

Black particles attracted to grid

Grid electrodes have negative charge

Grid electrodes have positive charge

Augmented reality

Using a smartphone, digital tablet, or similar device, an interactive environment of sound, music, photos, video, and text can blend with your surroundings to create a real-time, information-rich connection between you and the world. This is augmented reality (AR), an exciting area of development that may revolutionize how we relate to both technology and the world around us.

↗ How it works

There are different ways to create AR. Usually, though, an application scans an image or scene, then calls up additional information using a data connection.

● Many AR applications designed for use out and about exploit a mobile device's GPS (Global Positioning System) technology, internal compass or tracking sensors, and camera. Together, these can figure out where the device is, the direction it is facing, and what it is looking at.

● Linking to the Internet through dedicated databases or web searches, the AR application pulls up relevant information and other media, such as videos, to display as layers onscreen.

↗ AR applications

● Columbia University's ARMAR system is trialling AR in engineering. As a technician looks at a machine, labels of its parts and videos of repair and fitting techniques appear on the head-mounted display.

● In the future, social networking may get an AR makeover. Pointing your device at a person could match with photos of them on the Internet, to call up their Facebook page and Twitter account.

● AR books are already with us. When pointed at a webcam, they can link to the Internet to generate 3-D animations onscreen, such as a dinosaur roaming the page.

Landmarks
Local attractions are mapped and detailed. Unlike in a printed guidebook, the information can be truly up to the minute, giving the opening hours for that day, plus details of special exhibitions or events, and their availability.

Keizersgracht
0.6 km (0.4 miles)

Food and drink
Clicking on a food, drink, or accommodation icon calls up nearby restaurants, cafés, bars, hotels, and hostels. Automatic Internet links provide reviews, tips, and, in some cases, daily specials, discounts, and prices.

Landmarks   Restaurants   Banks

AR in Amsterdam

A tablet PC displays the AR app, Layar, and its view of part of the Dutch city of Amsterdam. Layar offers a range of kinds of information, from locating tweets from people nearby to pointing at a building to see if any companies inside have jobs on offer. The data is displayed as layers onscreen that can be turned on and off.

Just the beginning

Could this be the end of the handset? SixthSense can project a working phone or calculator number pad onto your hand. It is still in development, but in the future, wearable projecting AR devices may be used in education, the military, business, and just for fun.

Transport
To answer any transport queries, the app displays the nearest bus and tram stops and lists train times. In cities with cycle hire, you can locate your nearest hire point and find out how many bikes are available.

Car finder
3.4 km (2.1 miles)
(17 mins remaining)

🚗 Head north for 1 km (0.6 miles) until you reach a bridge.
🚗 Head east for 2.4 km (1.5 miles) until you reach your car.

Utilities
Useful applications include directing you back to your car, and helping you to find the nearest open chemist, free Wi-Fi, or locksmith. You can even point your camera at a public building to call up photos of the interior.

Visitor attractions
Themed tourist walk layers can give you interactive directions as you move around the city. Providing an audio and video guide, they can focus on a particular attraction, giving photos, Web links, and other details.

Centraal Station
2.0 km (1.2 miles)

Geln

Westwijk

| Car location | Transport | Wi-Fi | Shops | Toilets | Hotels |

From arcades to
consoles

Almost no one played video games in the 1960s. The first computer action game, 1961's *Space War!*, required access to a PDP-1 mainframe, which cost more than £75,000 (US$120,000) and was found only in a handful of large organizations. Fortunately, one of those organizations was the University of Utah, USA, where a young Nolan Bushnell was studying. He notched up plenty of playing hours and went on to pioneer the introduction of computer games into arcades and, later, people's homes.

Did you know?

As a science-mad teenager, Bushnell built a liquid-fuel rocket mounted on a roller skate. Unfortunately, it exploded and nearly burned down the family garage!

Nolan Bushnell

After studying electrical engineering at the University of Utah, Nolan Bushnell (born 1943) began working at Ampex, the electronics company that invented video tape. There, he met engineer Ted Dabney, with whom he formed Syzygy in 1971. The company changed its name to Atari the following year.

Arcade action

In 1970, Bushnell and Dabney began to develop an arcade game version of *Space War!*. The result, *Computer Space*, was brought out by Nutting Associates in 1971. It was the first mass-produced arcade computer game, with around 1,500 machines built.

Bushnell's workshop

After leaving Atari in 1978, Bushnell funded various companies, including Androbot, creators of robots. Bushnell rejoined Atari in 2010.

> "The simple, classic games, where we didn't have those graphics to fall back on, had to be really well-tuned, and the response times had to be honed. We focused more on game play than I think people do today."
>
> *Nolan Bushnell, 2009*

Pong

In September 1972, Atari produced its first arcade game, *Pong*. Bushnell and Dabney built the game using a shop-bought television, a coin mechanism from a launderette, and a milk carton inside to catch the coins. The debut machine was so popular that it overfilled with 25¢ coins and broke down. More than 30,000 *Pong* arcade machines would be sold.

Top-selling Atari 2600 games

1 *Pac-Man*
2 *Pitfall!*
3 *Missile Command*
4 *Demon Attack*
5 *E.T. the Extra-Terrestrial*
6 *Atlantis*
7 *Adventure*
8 *River Raid*
9 *Kaboom!*
10 *Space Invaders*

A console classic

In 1977, the Atari 2600 video console was launched with just 128 bytes of built-in memory (a CD contains more than 700 million). The machine came with two paddles (above), two joysticks, and a series of Combat shooting games. Further games were sold on cartridges containing just 4 K (later 16 K) of memory. After a slow start, sales boomed. In 1980, Atari notched up £1.25 billion (US$2 billion) of sales, including millions of consoles and games such as *Pac-Man*, *Space Invaders*, and *Pitfall!* – one of the first successful platform games.

Atari innovation

Atari was more than a one-trick pony. Its 400, 800, and XT home computers sold well, and the 1989 Atari Lynx (right) was the first hand-held games console with a backlit colour LCD screen. Able to link with and play against other machines, the Lynx was well ahead of its time but sold poorly compared to its main rival, the Game Boy.

Did you know?

The three founders of Apple – Steve Jobs, Steve Wozniak, and Ronald Wayne – all previously worked for Atari. Steve Wozniak developed the prototype of the smash-hit Atari game, Breakout.

Early games

On its release in 1981, the shoot 'em up game *Galaga* (below) with its blocky colour graphics, swooping streams of aliens, and chorus of bleeps coming from its one speaker was considered state of the art. Gaming has changed enormously since early arcade and home computers and consoles, yet those old games still keep their addictive appeal. On New Year's Day, 2011, Andrew Laidlaw set a *Galaga* world record tournament score of 4,525,150 points.

Arcade play

In the beginning, the only place most people were able to play electronic games was in a noisy arcade with crowds of others. You often had to queue for the most popular games, and needed a pocketful of the right coins.

Did you know?

The 1976 *Colossal Cave Adventure* had just 700 lines of game code and an additional 700 lines of data. The latest Assassin's Creed game, *Brotherhood* had a 600 page script and around 4 million lines of program code.

Game worlds

The game of *Galaga* was just a single screen down which different waves of aliens travelled. Like many early games, there were just three controls required – left, right, and fire. Both gameplay and game worlds have mushroomed in scale, size, and complexity since. *Anarchy Online*, for example, has a 112-page manual of instructions for its "getting started" section alone, whilst *Tiger Woods PGA Tour 11* includes accurate 3-D models of 27 complete real-life golf courses.

Sounds good

Early games were silent or merely bleeped. Then, in 1980, an arcade game called *Rally X*, became one of the first to feature background music. Later the same year the game *Stratovox* surprised players with voice-synthesized speech. Modern games have complex soundtracks and tens of thousands of lines of speech, far more than a typical movie.

1UP 00   HIGH SCORE 00

Great graphics

Processing power has increased sharply, and most modern computers and consoles feature high-speed graphics cards. Incredibly realistic 3-D worlds, scenes, and characters are now standard in many games.

GAME OVER

CREDIT 0

Did you know?

Space Invaders was so big in Japan in 1980 that there was a shortage of the coins used in arcade consoles. The government had to mint 200 million extra 100-yen coins to meet demand.

"When Taito saw the prototype (of *Space Invaders*), they said, 'You can't shoot people! And you must not create the image of war.' So I changed the characters into monsters. At the time, I was trying to decide what the focus would be, and had heard of a sci-fi movie being produced in America called *Star Wars*. I thought a space fad might be on the way and decided to focus on aliens. And that's how the monsters became the invaders that are known today."

Tomohiro Nishikado

Joining Japanese pinball and vending machine company Taito in 1969, Tomohiro Nishikado (born 1944) designed a number of Japan's early arcade games before releasing Space Invaders in 1978. One of the first addictive, action-shooter games, it caused a sensation and inspired other designers. Taito sold Space Invader consoles in Japan and the USA and then, in 1980, brought it into millions of homes by transfering the game to the Atari 2600 games console. It is still played today.

The story of Nintendo

Once upon a time, Nintendo was just a humble maker of playing cards in Kyoto, Japan. One hundred and twenty years later, it is one of its country's biggest success stories. It is a giant in the video games industry, with its products found in homes the world over. It's safe to say that Nintendo has played an important role in shaping the way that we interact with computer games today.

→ Donkey Kong
Where it all began in 1981! Created for arcade machines, *Donkey Kong* launched Miyamoto's career and kick-started Nintendo's dominance.

← NES
In 1983, the company's first cartridge game system, the Nintendo Entertainment System sold all over the world. It overtook the Atari 2600 as the market leader.

→ Super Mario
Originally named "Jumpman", Mario is arguably the world's most recognizable cartoon character – just as famous as Mickey Mouse.

↓ Pokémon
Since first appearing in 1996, games featuring these "pocket monsters" have together sold around 200 million copies.

Origins

People think of Nintendo as a cutting-edge company, but it was actually founded, in 1889, to manufacture cards for Hanafuda, a popular Japanese card game. In the 1960s, Nintendo branched out, running taxis and making instant rice meals. In the 1970s, it sold its first toys and video games. Nintendo produced its first hand-held electronic game, the Game & Watch, in 1980.

Shigeru Miyamoto

As the creator of *Donkey Kong*, Mario, *The Legend of Zelda*, and the Wii, Shigeru Miyamoto (born 1952) may be responsible for more man-hours lost to gaming than anyone in history! Miyamoto, who joined Nintendo as its first staff artist in 1977, is now responsible for every Nintendo game, and has been dubbed the "Walt Disney" of the video game industry.

Did you know?

Donkey Kong was supposedly based on the cartoon Popeye the Sailor Man. Miyamoto replaced Bluto with Donkey Kong, Olive with a princess, and Popeye himself with Mario!

↑ SNES
In 1990, the Super Nintendo Entertainment System arrived with double the processing power of the NES, allowing a big leap forwards in game quality.

Studio supervisor

Miyamoto's mentor was Gunpei Yokoi, originally hired by Nintendo in 1965 to repair conveyor belts and other assembly-line kit. Yokoi went on to invent the Game Boy as well as to supervise the making of both *Donkey Kong* and Mario.

→ Game Boy
Released in 1989 with the classic game *Tetris*, the Game Boy blasted away rival hand-held opposition. With more than 118 million sold, it's one of the bestselling gaming devices of all time.

→ GameCube
Launched in 2001, the GameCube was Nintendo's first console to use disks instead of cartridges.

← N64
Released in Japan in 1996, the N64 was the first 64-bit console in the world, and raised the standards for 3-D graphics.

→ The Legend of Zelda
Introduced in 1997, Link (right) is the main character in *The Legend of Zelda*. He has been trying to rescue Princess Zelda in 17 different games.

← Nintendo DS/DS Lite
The DS, launched in 2004, was the first device to have a microphone, built-in Wi-Fi, and dual screens, one of which had a touch interface.

→ Nintendo Wii
In 2006, Nintendo introduced the Wii, which brought motion control to games and introduced a whole new generation of people to video games.

↗ Nintendo by numbers

4,130
The number of people who are employed by Nintendo worldwide

649
The number of species of Pokémon

135.6 million
The number of DS machines sold worldwide from 2004 to October 2010

1 in 5
The number of people in Japan who own a model of the Nintendo DS

£9.5 billion
(US$15.2 billion) Nintendo's total revenue for 2009

1,068,000
The highest *Donkey Kong* score so far, achieved by 35-year-old plastic surgeon Hank Chien in 2011

25
The number of years since the release of the first *Super Mario* game

1st
Miyamoto's rank in *TIME Magazine*'s list of the world's 100 most influential people in 2008

2.5
The number of Nintendo consoles sold every second in the USA during Thanksgiving week (22–28 November) in 2009

Did you know?

Loosely translated, the Japanese word *nintendo* means "Leave luck to heaven".

The evolution of game controllers

Game controllers allow players to interact with and influence events on screen. Early games were slow-paced – with few moves available to the player, designers gave little thought to the quality or versatility of the controllers. As games have grown more complex, so have the ways to control them. There is now a multi-million-pound market for the game pads, force-feedback joysticks, and motion-sensing devices that give players the edge in split-second encounters.

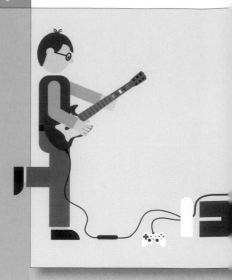

↗ **Specialist controllers**

Did you know?

A special, single-player controller was produced for the Japanese robot tanks game, *Steel Battalion*. It had two joysticks, three foot pedals, and 40 buttons.

Type it in

Once upon a time, home computer games used a humble keyboard as their controller. Text adventures called for phrases or sentences to be typed in. Today, there are dedicated gaming keyboards, such as the Razer BlackWidow, which are often backlit for use at night. Their keys are responsive and tough enough to take a pounding. Some can be programmed so that pressing one key has the same effect as pressing several other keys at once.

Paddles

Atari's ground-breaking early games, such as *Pong* and *Breakout*, were played with paddles – controllers featuring a turning wheel and one or more fire buttons. Each paddle allowed movement along one axis. The trackball was another controller used in early gaming, for example for the shoot-'em-up, *Centipede*. Similar to an upside-down mouse, it had a large ball that was rolled by hand to create movement along two axes.

Joysticks

Early joysticks were four-way movement controllers with a single fire button. Over time, these evolved into more complex and versatile devices. Modern joysticks boast multiple "hot" buttons that can be programmed to perform different game functions. Most joysticks have a hat switch on top of the handle. When activated, this can change the view – allowing the player to look around the game world, for example.

Some games require controllers that break the mould of game pads and joysticks. Here are some of the most popular ones.

Flight simulators
Mimicking the controls of a light aircraft, flight sims have a hand-operated control column and a foot-controlled rudder bar.

Voice control
Karaoke games, such as *SingStar*, rely on a microphone linked to the console to measure a player's singing prowess. Microphones are also used in war games such as *EndWar*, so that players can issue voice commands to their troops.

Musical instruments
Guitar Hero games have a guitar-shaped controller with five coloured fret buttons and a strum bar.

Dance mats
Mats fitted with pressure sensors allow people to play dance games, stepping in sync with the commands on the screen.

Balance boards
The Wii Fit balance board uses load sensors to detect a player's position and track movements as weight is shifted from one part of the board to another.

Steering wheels
Many driving games are controlled with a steering wheel. Some feature foot pedals, gearsticks, and indicators as well.

Did you know?
A limited edition of the third-person shooter *Resident Evil 4* came with a gruesome game pad in the shape of a bloodstained chainsaw.

ame pads

ame pads feature a series of action nd fire buttons around their body, long with a direction controller – sually a four-arrow D-pad (directional ad) or analog stick (a small, sensitive ystick). Game pads arrived once ame play demanded lots of options. ome feature force feedback, where otors make the game pad move or ibrate in the hand in response to ertain actions, such as when the layer fires a machine gun.

Motion sensors

The motion-sensing Wii remote (or Wiimote) contains accelerometers that detect changes in movement in three different axes (up and down, side to side, and forward and back). Accelerometers work whether the controller is held horizontally like a gun or vertically like a golf club. The system determines the exact position of the controller using beams of infrared light projected from the sensor bar next to the screen.

Your body!

Kinect for the Xbox 360 is the first in a new breed of hands-free controllers. It projects a continuous, coded infrared light beam across the playing space in front of the screen. Then it measures how the light returns in order to build up a 3-D picture of the playing area and any player movements. With a controller like Kinect, players can take part in games just by moving and making gestures. The device also responds to spoken commands.

Kinect

Nintendo's Wii laid down the motion sensing gauntlet to all-comers, but Kinect for the Xbox 360 is a whole different game. The device is a horizontal sensor bar which detects and measures a player's position and movements within a 3-D space in front of the screen. As a result, players can run, jump, throw, and play a new range of controller-free action-adventure, yoga, dance, and sports games.

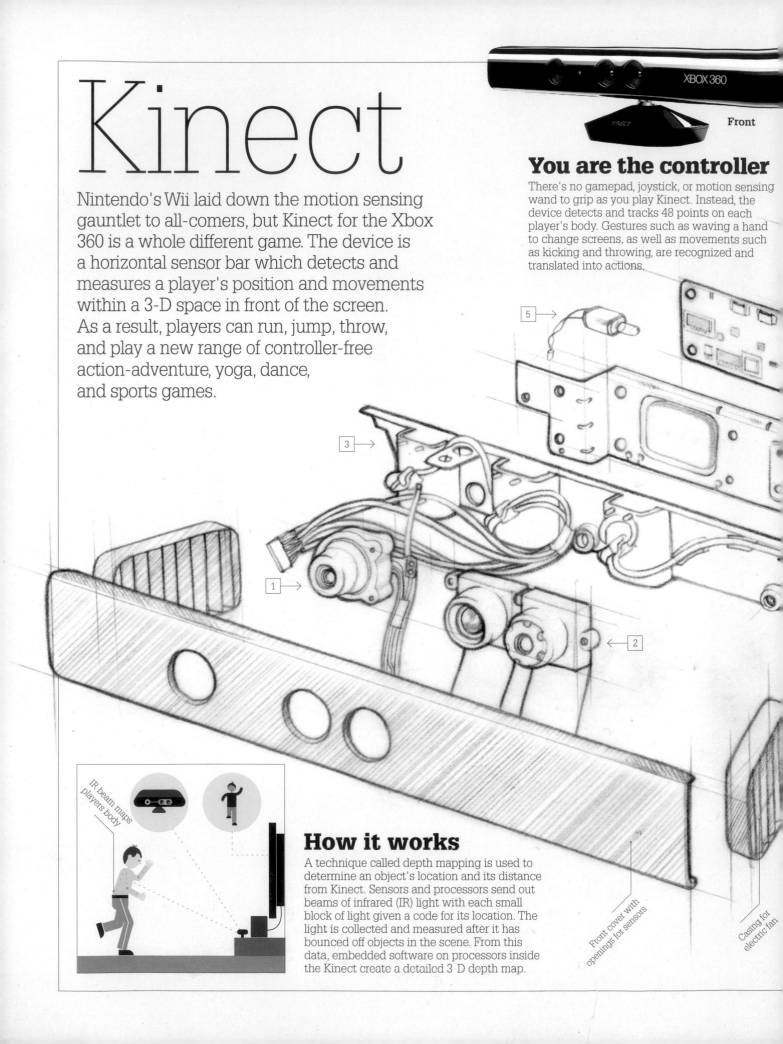

Front

You are the controller

There's no gamepad, joystick, or motion sensing wand to grip as you play Kinect. Instead, the device detects and tracks 48 points on each player's body. Gestures such as waving a hand to change screens, as well as movements such as kicking and throwing, are recognized and translated into actions.

5

3

1

2

How it works

A technique called depth mapping is used to determine an object's location and its distance from Kinect. Sensors and processors send out beams of infrared (IR) light with each small block of light given a code for its location. The light is collected and measured after it has bounced off objects in the scene. From this data, embedded software on processors inside the Kinect create a detailed 3-D depth map.

IR beam maps players' body

Front cover with openings for sensors

Casing for electric fan

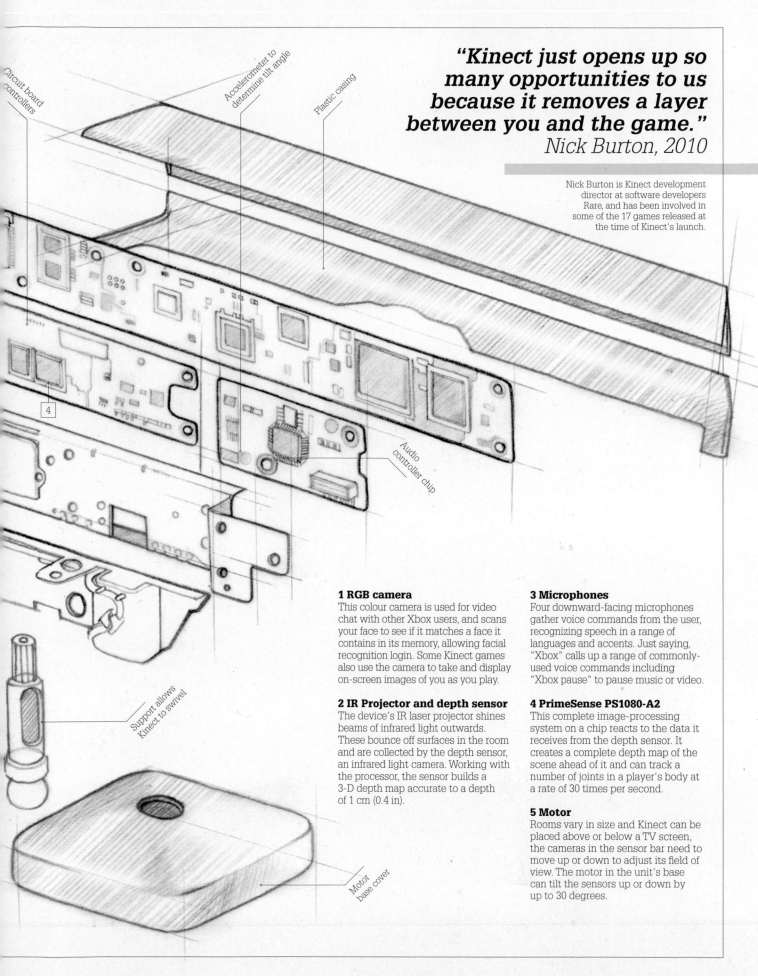

Circuit board controllers

Accelerometer to determine tilt angle

Plastic casing

4

Audio controller chip

Support allows Kinect to swivel

Motor base cover

"Kinect just opens up so many opportunities to us because it removes a layer between you and the game."
Nick Burton, 2010

Nick Burton is Kinect development director at software developers Rare, and has been involved in some of the 17 games released at the time of Kinect's launch.

1 RGB camera
This colour camera is used for video chat with other Xbox users, and scans your face to see if it matches a face it contains in its memory, allowing facial recognition login. Some Kinect games also use the camera to take and display on-screen images of you as you play.

2 IR Projector and depth sensor
The device's IR laser projector shines beams of infrared light outwards. These bounce off surfaces in the room and are collected by the depth sensor, an infrared light camera. Working with the processor, the sensor builds a 3-D depth map accurate to a depth of 1 cm (0.4 in).

3 Microphones
Four downward-facing microphones gather voice commands from the user, recognizing speech in a range of languages and accents. Just saying, "Xbox" calls up a range of commonly-used voice commands including "Xbox pause" to pause music or video.

4 PrimeSense PS1080-A2
This complete image-processing system on a chip reacts to the data it receives from the depth sensor. It creates a complete depth map of the scene ahead of it and can track a number of joints in a player's body at a rate of 30 times per second.

5 Motor
Rooms vary in size and Kinect can be placed above or below a TV screen, the cameras in the sensor bar need to move up or down to adjust its field of view. The motor in the unit's base can tilt the sensors up or down by up to 30 degrees.

07:00

13:00

1 Connecting

Players join a game by subscribing or paying a set fee. They download software onto their computer, known as "the client". Before play can begin, the client must connect to a server.

2 Sending

The client computer's signal travels across the world via fibre-optic cable until it reaches the server. Then the server sends a signal back to the client computer, informing the player that a connection has been established.

Did you know?

EVE Online is a space game where players explore a universe of more than 7,500 star systems. On 6 June 2010, more than 60,000 players were all logged on to *EVE* at the same time.

Client

North America

Relay point

Limiting lag

Lag is when messages take too lo[ng] to reach all the clients. Lengthy la[g] can be lethal in quick-fire combat games. Players limit lag by makin[g] sure their computers run fast and logging on only to speedy servers that offer a good connection.

Relay point

South America

→ Playing together

Not so long ago, if you wanted to play a computer game with or against other people, they had to be in the same room. Today, you can play as a wizard or warlord in Washington, Wisconsin, or Warsaw and battle adversaries in Africa, Asia, or Australia. Millions of players around the world are ready to join you or play against you in thousands of online, multi-player games. All you and they require is a computer or gaming device that is connected to the game's network.

Did you know?

In the two years after the release of action game *Halo 2*, more than four billion games were played on its servers worldwide, almost 5.5 million games a day.

20:30

00:00

3 Distributing

As the game is played, players' locations and actions are tracked by the game server. When a player moves, fires a weapon, or types a message to another player, an update or "state-of-the-world" message is sent to the server.

5 Sending back

The other players' responses travel back to the server and the process begins all over again. All of this takes place in a split second, and it carries on happening every second of the day.

Europe

Asia

Server

Relay point

Relay point

Africa

4 Receiving

The state-of-the-world messages are sent to all players logged into the game. The client computers immediately process the messages and produce graphics, text, and sound to show the latest actions onscreen. Then the other players can respond to what they see.

On and on...

The game featured here runs on a centralized server that is operational 24 hours a day, allowing players to come and go. As Australian gamers finally head off to bed, American players may just be getting up and logging on.

Australia

↗ Distributed servers

Complex games, particularly pacy action games such as *Halo* that require frequent status messages, spread the load across multiple smaller servers rather than just one centralized server. When players log on to the game, a master server provides a list of available smaller servers for the client to connect to in order to play.

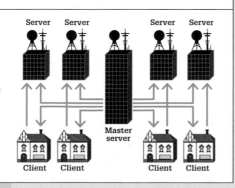

Server   Server   Server   Server

Master server

Client   Client   Client   Client

How video games are made

That disk you slide into your games console is the product of huge teams and big budgets. When *Doom* was released in 1993, industry insiders were stunned that a game could cost £136,000 (US$200,000) to make. A modern game budget can be 200 times that. To produce the smash shooter, *Call of Duty: Black Ops*, game developers Teyarch had 250 staff working for two years

The design doc 2
A comprehensive design document is put together, containing the core game details, features, and deadlines. Games can spend a long time in development. Maxis' 2008 game, *Spore*, took nine years.

The storyboard 3
The characters, worlds, scenes, and endings are sketched out and, later, scripted and graphics-choreographed.

The pitch 1
At meetings, meetings, and more meetings, the developers (the company that will construct the game) pitch their idea to the publishers (the company that will market the finished game).

Engines and coding 4
The games engine is the core software that handles how 3-D graphics are rendered onscreen. Many games use off-the-shelf engines, but that still leaves thousands of lines of program code to be written.

Did you know?

↗ ESRB ratings

The USA is the biggest gaming market, so developers take its product ratings very seriously. Of the 1,791 games rated by the US Entertainment Software Rating Board (ESRB) in 2009:

60% received an E (Everyone) rating

16% received an E10+ (Everyone 10+) rating

18% received a T (Teen) rating

6% received an M (Mature) rating for adults only

No small task

More than 1,000 staff worked on *Grand Theft Auto 4*. Tasks ranged from studying New York traffic patterns for realism, to contacting more than 2,000 people to secure the rights to the music that makes up the soundtrack. The game took three-and-a-half years to make and cost around £52 million (US$100 million).

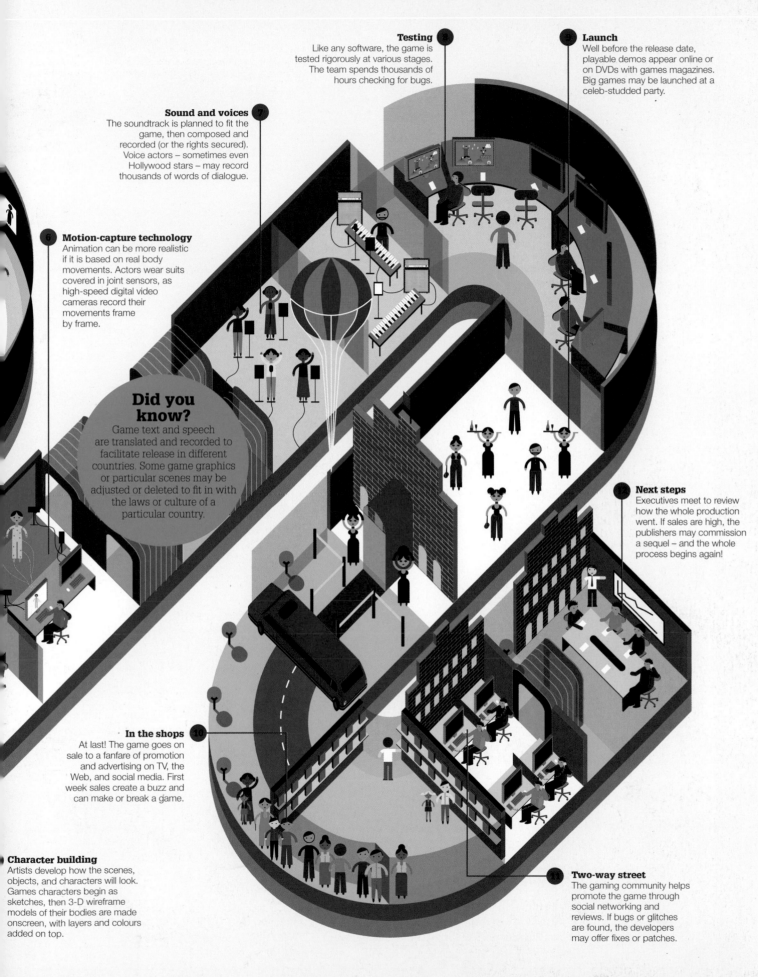

Testing ⑧
Like any software, the game is tested rigorously at various stages. The team spends thousands of hours checking for bugs.

Launch ⑨
Well before the release date, playable demos appear online or on DVDs with games magazines. Big games may be launched at a celeb-studded party.

Sound and voices ⑦
The soundtrack is planned to fit the game, then composed and recorded (or the rights secured). Voice actors – sometimes even Hollywood stars – may record thousands of words of dialogue.

⑥ **Motion-capture technology**
Animation can be more realistic if it is based on real body movements. Actors wear suits covered in joint sensors, as high-speed digital video cameras record their movements frame by frame.

Did you know?
Game text and speech are translated and recorded to facilitate release in different countries. Some game graphics or particular scenes may be adjusted or deleted to fit in with the laws or culture of a particular country.

Next steps ⑫
Executives meet to review how the whole production went. If sales are high, the publishers may commission a sequel – and the whole process begins again!

In the shops ⑩
At last! The game goes on sale to a fanfare of promotion and advertising on TV, the Web, and social media. First week sales create a buzz and can make or break a game.

Character building
Artists develop how the scenes, objects, and characters will look. Games characters begin as sketches, then 3-D wireframe models of their bodies are made onscreen, with layers and colours added on top.

Two-way street ⑪
The gaming community helps promote the game through social networking and reviews. If bugs or glitches are found, the developers may offer fixes or patches.

Role-playing games

Known as RPGs, these complex games prove highly addictive to loyal gamers, who generally control a group, or party, of characters on various quests. Most RPGs are set in fantasy worlds or sci-fi settings. Online RPGs with huge followings, such as *World of Warcraft*, are known as MMORPGs – massively multiplayer online role-playing games.

Platform games

In the 1980s and early '90s, about a fifth of all games sold were platform games, featuring characters that leap between suspended platforms or over obstacles in different scenes. From *Jet Set Willy* and *Donkey Kong* to various Sonic and Mario games, including *Super Mario 64* with its 3-D game play, platforms are especially popular on hand-held consoles.

Racing games

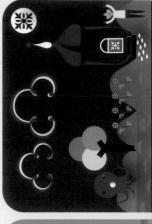

Racing sped out of the arcades into homes on consoles and computers and is popular with all ages. Games such as *Forza Motorsport*, *SBK-09*, and the *Gran Turismo* series pride themselves on racing realism, using accurate models of vehicles and famous race circuits. Others, such as *Mario Kart* and *Konami Krazy Racers*, are more fantasy-based.

Simulations

A sim is a game that allows you to simulate an activity. These range from looking after virtual pets, to flight simulators, and sports management games. Others simulate life evolving over several generations, or let you build a virtual home, town, or world. With more than 90 million units sold, *The Sims* is the biggest-selling simulation series ever.

Games of strategy

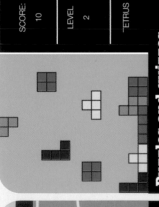

Strategy games are usually turn-based, tactical games between two players or one player and the computer. They include board games, such as chess, war games, such as *Command & Conquer* and *Total War*, and the legendary *Civilization* series, which includes *Civilization V* for PCs and the Internet MMORPG, *Civilization World*.

Third-person shooters

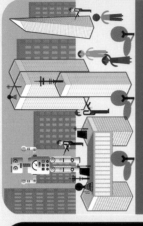

From *Space Invaders* onwards, gamers have loved third-person shooters, where they control a character moving through a game world in the near distance. This figure interacts with objects or other characters and, of course, fires all sorts of weaponry. Enemies may range from plague-infested zombies (*Resident Evil*) to armed aliens (*Gears of War*).

Puzzles and quizzes

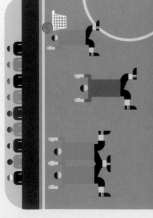

Games that challenge and train your brain come in a range of formats, from online and hand-held trivia quizzes to graphic puzzles and cryptic word games. Not one is more famous than Alexey Pajitnov's 1984 creation, *Tetris*. More than 100 million copies of the falling-blocks puzzle game have been sold for mobile phones alone since 2005.

Competitive sports

Many new consoles launch with free sports titles, to attract buyers. From basketball to big bass fishing, these games are hugely popular, particularly with casual gamers. Many top games feature real-life sporting champions. The best-selling sports game franchise to date is the *EA Sports FIFA* series, which has sold more than 65 million copies.

What do you want to play?

Like a shape-shifting monster in a sci-fi world, game types keep changing and evolving. In the distant past, they fell into just two types: slow-moving strategy or adventure games, and arcade games requiring quick reactions. Now games are incredibly involved and complex. *Gran Turismo 4*, for instance, has 721 cars available to customize and drive. Today there are many different game genres. Here are a dozen of the most popular types.

Adventure games

Beginning with text-only games in the 1970s, adventures place the gamer in a world to explore. They involve meeting characters and objects, collecting clues, solving puzzles, and finding new places. Gently-paced, early adventures such as *Zork* attracted new players to gaming. Compelling games such as *Myst* and *Fahrenheit* have kept the genre going.

First-person shooters

These shooting games place you right in the action, looking at the game world through your character's eyes. They got a massive boost with the arrival of 3-D graphics in games such as *Wolfenstein 3-D* and *Doom*. Some games, such as *Halo: Reach*, have detailed stories and such high levels of graphic violence that they have an adult-only rating.

Fighting games

In the 1980s, most fighting games were beat-'em-ups, in which a character had to punch, kick, and knock out swarms of opponents. The release of *Street Fighter II* in 1991 saw a shift towards one-on-one fighting, continued by *Mortal Kombat*, *Virtua Fighter*, and *Tekken*. Pressing multiple buttons at speed produces a range of martial-arts-inspired moves.

Got rhythm?

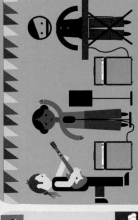

First seen in Japanese arcades, dancing games such as *Dance Dance Revolution* and *Pump It Up* test a player's rhythm and timing as they try to copy onscreen dance moves. They were followed by games allowing players to show off their musical skills, including *Guitar Hero* and the unusual *Donkey Konga*, which has a pair of bongos as the game controller.

Did you know?

In September 2003, Tell Quest became the first British cellphone playing *Terravin* its mobile phone on an airwall. This is Special 9e6: broadcast of tele-services via broadcast communications

Console wars

A battle is raging for world supremacy. To the victor goes untold millions, make that billions, of dollars and dominance. To the loser may go defeat, large losses, and a retreat from the games console arena. Welcome to the console wars – a fierce competition for increased market share between games machines. At the start of 2011, it's a seventh-generation, head-to-head battle between Microsoft's Xbox 360, Sony's PlayStation 3, and Nintendo's Wii.

Did you know?

For much of the 1990s, Sega was a key player in the console wars. However, several poor-selling machines in a row saw the home of Sonic the Hedgehog move out of consoles and into computer software by 2001.

Spectrum vs C64

One of the first games wars occured in the UK in the 1980s between the Sinclair Spectrum and Commodore C64 computers. Millions of games were sold for both machines.

Home grown

Although the Wii is the bestselling machine in the Americas, with nearly half the market share, the home grown Xbox 360 also does well, generating nearly 59 per cent of total Xbox sales.

45.3%

33.9%

20.8%

Most ever?

The PS2, first released in 2000, is the most successful console of all time with more than 140 million sold. It is still going strong. In 2010, Sony launched an HD television with a built-in PS2.

Who's winning where?

Consoles have varying popularity in different regions for several reasons. Sony, for example, publish many games that have been historically tailored to the Japanese market, whereas the types of game typically played by Westerners are more popular on the Xbox. As for the Wii, it's popular everywhere!

Sony PlayStation 3	**46.99 million worldwide**
Nintendo Wii	**84.48 million worldwide**
Microsoft Xbox 360	**51.15 million worldwide**

Americas

While Brazil and Mexico are growing national markets, the USA is where the big money is to be had. In 2008, the US games industry was worth more than £7.3 billion (US$11.7 billion) of revenue – equal to 195 million copies of the *Call of Duty: Black Ops* game or 3.3 million PS3 consoles.

Wii world conquest

At the moment the Wii is winning. It's the biggest-selling console in each region and makes up nearly half of all consoles sold worldwide. That's a big turnaround from 2002 when Nintendo's GameCube slumped a distant third behind the original Xbox and PlayStation. The secret? The Wii's mix of innovative, motion-sensing controllers and family titles that attract gamers of all ages. But it's not all over yet. In 2010, both Sony with Move and Microsoft with Kinect (see page 90) launched motion-sensing competitors.

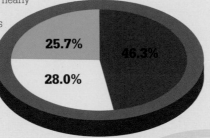

25.7% **46.3%** **28.0%**

PlayStation	Wii	Xbox 360
£310–375 million (US$500–$600 million)	£30–90 million (US$49-$149 million)	£750 million (US$1,200 million)

Online revenue

Console manufacturers are making more and more money from online services, such as downloadable content, upgrades, in-game items, and subscription services. Microsoft leads the way with its Xbox Live subscription, which as of 2011 had more than 30 million members.

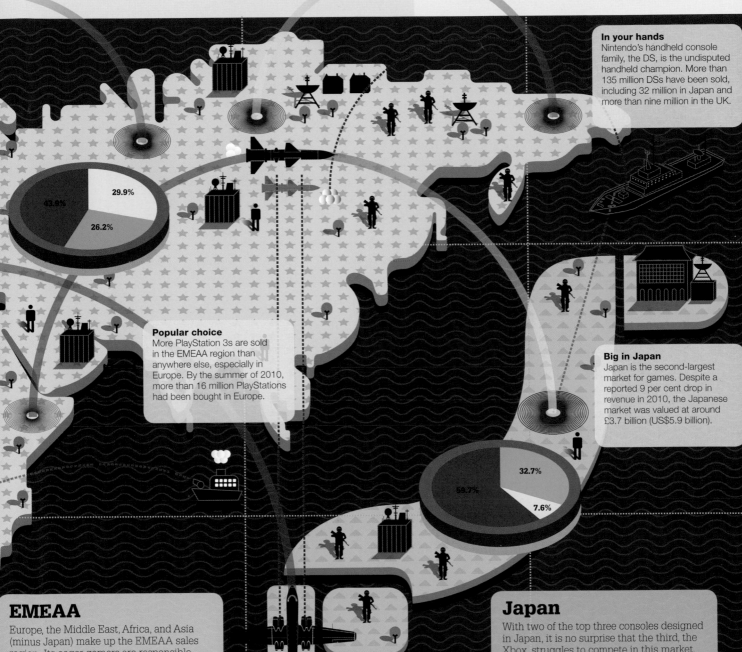

In your hands
Nintendo's handheld console family, the DS, is the undisputed handheld champion. More than 135 million DSs have been sold, including 32 million in Japan and more than nine million in the UK.

43.9% **29.9%** **26.2%**

Popular choice
More PlayStation 3s are sold in the EMEAA region than anywhere else, especially in Europe. By the summer of 2010, more than 16 million PlayStations had been bought in Europe.

Big in Japan
Japan is the second-largest market for games. Despite a reported 9 per cent drop in revenue in 2010, the Japanese market was valued at around £3.7 billion (US$5.9 billion).

59.7% **32.7%** **7.6%**

EMEAA

Europe, the Middle East, Africa, and Asia (minus Japan) make up the EMEAA sales region. Its eager gamers are responsible for 40 per cent of worldwide Wii, PS3, and Xbox 360 sales. No major consoles are made in the EMEAA, but plenty of games are developed by companies from these areas.

Japan

With two of the top three consoles designed in Japan, it is no surprise that the third, the Xbox, struggles to compete in this market. Sony and Nintendo duel both in the main console market and in a separate handheld battle between the DS family and Sony's Playstation Portable (PSP).

N

Virtual worlds

Role-playing games (RPGs) have been popular ever since computers were first networked together. Controlling their character, players take part in a story, quest, or adventure set in a virtual world. Players must make hundreds of decisions as they interact with other players, as well as game characters not controlled by players. The largest RPG games, Massively Multiplayer Online Role-Playing Games (MMORPGs), are hugely popular, with millions of participants.

MUD

In **1978**, *MUD*, short for **"Multi-User Dungeon"** went online. It is considered the first multiplayer online game. *MUD* was a text adventure game where users picked up points for collecting treasure and dropping it into a swamp, or for killing other players. Despite access to the game being rare in the early eighties, by 1984, more than **20,000 playing hours** had been notched up in *MUD*.

Kesmai

In 1985, a multiplayer online game called **Island of Kesmai** was launched, a forerunner of today's MMORPGs. Players had to pay **£6 (US$12.00) per hour** for connection to the game. *Island of Kesmai* supported up to 100 users playing at the same time. Today, *World of Warcraft* can have more than **a million people playing at one time**.

 **Lives**

Runescape

With more than **10 million active users**, *Runescape* is the world's largest free MMORPG. It began in 2001, developed by two brothers, Andrew and Paul Gower, and was initially run from their parents' house in Nottingham, UK. *Runescape* players chat, trade, can go on quests or enter different types of combat with other players. Now run by Jagex, up to **340,000 people** can enter the fantasy world of Gielinor and play simultaneously.

Hattrick

RPGs are not all about slaying warlocks or battling alien hordes. Hattrick is a soccer management MMORPG in which players buy and sell players, and employ a range of tactics as they try to outsmart other teams. Launched in Sweden in 1997, it had more than **800,000 players** by 2010.

NetEase

Many games charge a subscription to play, which means serious money. Chinese company NetEase, current operator of *World of Warcraft* in China, received **£900 million (US$1.59 billion)** in online game revenues in three months in 2009.

Second Life

Launched by the company Linden Lab in 2003, *Second Life* is an MMORPG with its own economy and three landmasses to travel between.

Second Life players can own land and build their own objects from cubes and even start their own businesses. In 2006, Ailen Greff (as her *Second Life* avatar (character) Anshe Chung) became the first virtual US dollar millionaire, mainly through buying and selling land inside *Second Life*.

Goods and services in *Second Life* are paid for in Linden dollars which can be bought using real US dollars. In 2010, **L$255** equalled 60p (US$1).

£180

The price a premium member of *Second Life* needs to buy their first 65,536-sq-m (705,000-sq-ft) plot of virtual land is £180 (US$295).

28,274,505

The number of hours players spent in *Second Life* during the month of January 2008.

481 million hours

The number of hours people spent inside the world of *Second Life* in 2009.

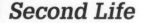

World of Warcraft

The biggest MMORPG on the planet is *World of Warcraft (WoW)*, a fantasy role playing game with over 60% of the total number of MMORPG gamers. In 2010, more than **12 million gamers** paid a subscription to play *WoW*.

WoW players by continent in 2010

22% North America

17% Europe

48% Asia

13% Other

WoW in numbers

1,400+
Locations to travel to

1,000+
Spells and skills to master

700
Different swords to wield

150
Books within the game to collect and read

5,300
NPCs (non player characters)

12,000
Types of beasts and enemies to slay or flee from

One in five *World of Warcraft* players is female.

20,000
The number of computer systems running some 5.5 million lines of code that make *WoW* possible.

3.3 million
The number of copies of PC game *WoW: Cataclysm* sold on its first day of release in 2010 – the fastest-selling PC game of all time.

4,600
The number of staff that work on *World of Warcraft*.

BIG WINNERS
World of Warcraft now runs online tournaments with cash prizes for the victors. At the 2010 *WoW* Global Arena tournament, there was prize money of **£124,000** (US$200,000), with **£46,000** (US$75,000) going to the winner.

Score: 128895

Gaming addiction

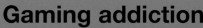

- With their ever-changing worlds and evolving characters, MMORPG gamers can get over-absorbed in the experience. For some, the games can prove seriously addictive. Treatment centres for game addicts have opened in China, South Korea, the Netherlands, and the USA.

- In 2006, a law was introduced in China limiting online gamers under the age of 18 to three hours continuous play in one go.

- South Korean MMORPG addict, Seungseob Lee, died in 2005 after playing *Starcraft* in an Internet café without rest for more than 40 hours.

Video games arrive

Computer technicians wrote primitive versions of chess and draughts in the 1950s, but it wasn't until the 1970s that gaming took off. Video-game fans still hung out in arcades, but gaming was also possible at home on computers and games consoles. Since then, each new generation of console has brought greater graphics and amazing new games.

Did you know?

In May 2004, Sony announced that the PlayStation had sold 100 million units worldwide, the first console in history to do so.

↓ 1974
Game company Atari release a home version of *Pong* and the first arcade racing game, *Gran Trak 10*.

↓ 1980
Pac-Man arrives in arcades, courtesy of the Japanese company, Namco. It is the first video game with a named, animated hero and becomes hugely popular with female as well as male gamers.

1984
While working at Moscow's Dorodnicyn Computing Centre, Alexey Pajitnov creates *Tetris*. The falling puzzle-block game is a huge success, helping launch the Game Boy and selling 100 million copies for mobile phones alone.

1961
Students at US university MIT write the program code for *Spacewar!* – the first computer action game featuring two battling spaceships. It runs the following year on a computer costing more than £75,000 (US$120,000).

↓ 1977
Atari launches the 2600, its first games console, one of the first to use cartridges.

1982
Microsoft releases *Flight Simulator 1.0.*, taking the quality and graphics for such games to new levels.

↓ 1988
The Sega Mega Drive (called the Sega Genesis in the USA) is released.

1952
British computer scientist AS Douglas produces *OXO*, a simple noughts and crosses computer game, at Cambridge University.

1975
US computer programmer William Crowther writes *Colossal Cave Adventure*, the first text adventure game for computers.

1987
The very first *Final Fantasy* game debuts in Japan. The *Final Fantasy* series would popularize graphic role-playing games.

↓ 1981
A vintage year for classic games with the arrivals of *Donkey Kong* and the Mario character (known as Jumpman). Mario has since appeared in 116 different computer games – the most by a single game character.

↑ 1989
Nintendo launches its first Game Boy. This, and the late colour version, will together s more than 118 million units and have hundreds of differe games designed for them.

↑ 1972
The world's first home gaming console, the Magnavox Odyssey, originally designed by US inventor Ralph Baer in the late 1960s, goes on sale.

↑ 1978
Space Invaders debuts in Japan's arcades. Its addictive game play and high score feature make it a major hit.

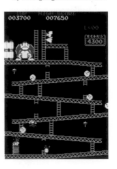

↑ 1983
The Nintendo Entertainment System (NES) range of games consoles begins production in Japan. Hugely influential, the consoles are manufactured for the next 20 years.

1989
US game designer Will Wright creates the city-building simulation game, *Sim City*. Wright will go on to create a whole series of related games.

3-D master

Graphics in games remained blocky and flat until the arrival of 3-D gaming. One of the key people responsible was John D Carmack, co-founder of id Software. Lead programmer on such ground-breaking games as *Wolfenstein 3D* and the *Doom* and *Quake* series, Carmack pioneered techniques to render graphics more quickly and make scenes more realistic, popularizing first-person shooters. His game engines have also been used on titles, such as *Call of Duty* and *Half-Life*.

"There are a lot of people [in the gaming industry] because they love games… Graphics and games are probably the most generally rewarding area of programming."

John D Carmack, 2000, US game programmer

1993
US company id Software releases *Doom*, a first-person shooter set in a fully 3-D environment, and with graphic violence. The game becomes both controversial and phenomenally popular.

↓ 1999
Sega launches its final console, the Dreamcast. It is discontinued just 2 years later.

↑ 2004
Nintendo release a handheld console, the DS. A month later Sony's PlayStation Portable (PSP) (above) is released in Japan, launching in the USA and Europe the following year.

→ 2010
The Kinect motion-sensing device for Xbox 360 offers controller-free gaming on some titles, operated by the player's body movements and voice commands.

1991
The Japanese company Sega brings out *Sonic the Hedgehog* and adopts the game's hedgehog hero as its company mascot.

→ 1996
Lara Croft stars in the original *Tomb Raider* game for the PlayStation.

2004
World of Warcraft debuts and becomes the world's most-played MMORPG.

2007
On its first day of release in the USA, the Xbox 360 game *Halo 3* generates £105 million (US$170 million) in sales.

1997
Fantasy game *Ultima Online* debuts – one of the first of the MMORPGs (massively multiplayer online role-playing games). It attracts more than 100,000 paid subscribers in less than 6 months.

↑ 2001
The US company Microsoft enters the games console market with the Xbox, the first major games console to contain an internal hard disk drive.

→ 2006
Sony releases the PS3 console as a rival to the recently released Xbox 360.

↑ 1994
Japanese company Sony launches its first PlayStation – a console that uses CDs instead of cartridges.

1992
Virtua Racing, released on Sega arcade consoles and later on home machines, offers exciting 3-D graphics viewable from different angles, as well as a force-feedback steering wheel, which handles like a real one.

1994
With violence in some games rising, the Entertainment Software Rating Board (ESRB) is established in North America to give ratings based on content.

1997
Final Fantasy VII is released to rave reviews. The quality of its graphics sets new standards for game design.

← 2006
Nintendo introduces the Wii. With its motion-sensitive Wii remote and multi-player games, it attracts millions of new casual gamers.

Digital camera

Digital cameras focus light through a lens onto an electronic image sensor made up of a grid of thousands of microscopic photosites. These convert the light energy into electrical energy, which is processed inside the camera's electronics to produce an image that you can save to memory, and later print, email or upload to a photo-sharing site.

Eyecup

Mode dial to
select shooting
modes

⟦1⟧

⟦2⟧

⟦3⟧

⟦4⟧

⟦5⟧

Playback button to
review pictures

CMOS sensor

LCD settings panel

Main dial to
adjust settings

Battery
compartment

Top

Back

Canon EOS 5D

This high quality digital SLR (single lens reflex), designed for serious photographers, stores its photos on CompactFlash memory cards. Its image sensor can capture images with a resolution of up to 4368 x 2912 pixels.

"They said digital would kill photography because everyone can do it... It makes photography interesting because everyone thinks they can take a picture."
David Bailey, 2006

David Bailey is an award-winning English photographer and photojournalist.

1 Viewfinder
The viewfinder of an SLR camera obtains a through-the-lens view, by using a mirror to direct the image from the lens up to the viewfinder. When an image is taken, the mirror flips up, allowing light to hit the sensor instead.

2 LCD display
Measuring 6cm (2.5 in) diagonally, the rear LCD (liquid crystal display) screen is made up of some 230,000 pixels. It can display menu and setting options but also allows you to review pictures immediately after they are taken.

3 Mainboard
The camera's mainboard contains its image processors and associated control microchips. The DIGIC II image processor receives electrical signals from the sensor and processes them into an image that is saved to memory.

4 Hot shoe
This bracket accepts the base of an external mountable flash gun – used to produce a flash of additional light in time with the camera shutter opening to obtain a bright image in dark or low light conditions.

5 Shutter release button
The camera's shutter opens and closes rapidly, allowing a precise amount of light in to hit the sensor. Slow shutter speeds create motion blur, while fast shutter speeds are used to capture and freeze motion.

6 Lens mount
The lens mount allows a lens to firmly click into place. It aligns electrical contacts from the camera and lens so that when camera is set to autofocus it can instruct the motors in the lens to turn to focus the image.

Lens
This 50 mm lens is described as prime or fixed, meaning it cannot change how closely it views the scene. Zoom lenses, however, can zoom in closer or further away from the subject.

7 Focus mode switch
Powered by a motor, the lens can be focused automatically by the camera For more creative control, the photographer can focus by hand after flicking the switch to manual.

8 Focusing ring
This control allows the photographer to focus the lens manually by turning the ring until the image looks sharp, either through the viewfinder or on the rear LCD screen.

9 Lens thread
A screw thread allows circular glass filters to be screwed on the front of the lens. Filters protect the lens and can enhance images by letting more or less of particular frequencies of light in.

CMOS sensor
The Canon EOS 5D uses a CMOS (complementary metal oxide semiconductor) sensor to capture images. Light focused by the lens reaches the sensor's surface where it is converted into electrical signals and sent to the camera's image processor.

Lenses work together to focus image

Front lens collects light from scene

Mirror

Rechargeable Battery

Battery flap

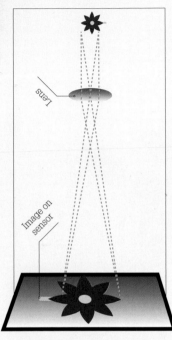

Lens

Image on sensor

Digital photography

Before the arrival of digital cameras, most cameras used a strip of chemically-coated film that reacted with light to create a photograph. Digicams have since taken over, built into everything from children's toys and mobile phones to the high-quality SLR (single-lens reflex) cameras used by professional photographers. For many, the best features of digital photography are that images can be manipulated and transmitted via the Internet.

↗ Image storage

The most popular film format was 35 mm, which came in rolls of 12 to 39 exposures (images). Digicams store photos as image files, usually on memory cards. A 4-GB Secure Digital (SD) card, a common size, can hold more than 1,000 images. The largest SD cards at 2 Terabytes are 512 times larger.

↗ The digital darkroom

Film photographers could develop their images in light-free darkrooms. Serious digital photographers use their computers as darkrooms. Photo-imaging software can alter lighting, remove blemishes, and apply effects. Then, the final image is printed out on a photo-quality printer.

A morphing filter pulls
the image out of shape.

A colour filter gives
the image a red tint.

A mosaic filter breaks up
the image into small tiles.

In-camera editing

Many digicams allow users to edit and alter an image while it is still held in the camera's memory. This can involve changing the colour or exposure level, cropping in close, or applying special effects filters – for example, to transform a colour photo into a sepia one or apply a texture like that of a painting.

Quality photographs

Digicams give more control. Users can determine the quality and file size of their images and delete pictures they don't like. The quality of the final image depends on various factors, including the camera's image-sensor resolution, often measured in megapixels (millions of pixels), and the quality of the lens. However, as with film photography, the most crucial ingredient is the skill of the person taking the picture.

Did you know?

An increasing number of digicams have built-in Wi-Fi. Users can upload their snaps to a website straight from the camera.

Digital images online

Stored as computer files, digital images are easy to email to others or upload onto the Internet. Online apps allow users to play with their photos, turning them into game avatars or personalized greeting cards. Photographers can sell their images through online image libraries or share them on photo sites, such as Flickr, Snapfish, Picasa, and Photobucket.

flickr

Search   Photos Groups People

Everyone's uploads   Giraffe   Search

it's going to appear pretty crazy to almost everybody. Either you do it yourself or it ain't going to happen."

Did you know?

At the age of 12, Sinclair designed an underwater submarine, and at 19, his IQ was measured at 159 (genius level). He was president of British Mensa, the high IQ society, from 1980 to 1997.

Clive Sinclair

Fascinated with shrinking technology and making it more affordable, English inventor Sir Clive Sinclair (born 1940) developed matchbox-sized radios, pocket TVs, pioneering digital watches, and, in 1972, the world's first pocket calculator. In 1980, he introduced the world's smallest, cheapest computer, the ZX80, followed by the bestselling ZX81 and Spectrum home computers. Despite the failure of his C5 electric vehicle, Sinclair continued to invent unusual vehicles, including tiny folding bikes and the SeaScooter underwater transporter.

Wired cities

While some parts of the world struggle for Internet access and remain on the wrong side of the digital divide, others are thriving. Their governments and industries have invested heavily to provide fast, plentiful, and free (or relatively cheap) broadband, Wi-Fi hotspots, and strong mobile phone links. There are also schemes to help people get the very most out of the available technology. In the world's most wired cities, information is never more than a mouse click or a touchscreen tap away.

Seoul, South Korea

Seoul is the world's most wired city. More than 93 per cent of its households have broadband. In many countries, broadband runs at 10–50 megabits per second (Mbps). By 2012, Seoul's broadband will run at 1,000 Mbps. The city is home to electronics giant, Samsung. Other companies at the cutting edge of technology, including Microsoft, Nokia, and Cisco, use Seoul as a living laboratory, testing many new products there before releasing them worldwide.

Always in touch
A girl uses the touchscreen of an Irobi personal robot in a Seoul department store. South Korea is home to many manufacturers of high-tech products. Its capital was the first city in the world to run a Digital Mobile Broadcasting (DMB) scheme, bringing TV stations and other services direct to mobile phones.

Did you know?

Seoul plans to become even more wired. Its Ubiquitous Seoul or U-City project plans to link everyone and everything electronically. Computer networks will control the appliances in smart apartments, while smartcards will track individual travellers via radio waves.

Tallinn, Estonia

The capital of Estonia is a beautiful medieval city, which just happens to be one of the most wired in Europe. Every seat in the parliament and town hall features a laptop, most bank transactions are performed online, and Estonians pay for travel tickets and parking fines using their mobile phones.

Seattle, USA

The northern seaport of Seattle is home to Microsoft, Amazon, the enormous digital picture library Getty Images, and a host of other high-tech companies. The city boasts powerful broadband access, which is provided free to local community groups, as well as Wi-Fi on buses and in parks.

A number of different forms of signal can now be used to control appliances remotely, from infrared for your television remote to Bluetooth on mobile phones and some laptops. Exciting applications are now applying remote control over long distances. They use the Internet to carry commands and deliver them to personal robots and other Wi-Fi-enabled devices.

→ Remote robot
This WowWee Rovio mobile webcam relies on Wi-Fi. It can send images to and be controlled by a user from anywhere in the world, as long as they have an Internet-enabled device.

Interacting with new technology

Technology is changing all around us and the old ways of controlling it may have to move aside. If even more technologies are to become part of our lives, and work seamlessly with us, devices and systems will need to offer simpler, more convenient, intuitive, and rewarding ways of interacting with them.

← Radio control
A child uses a radio transmitter to fly a glider. When the glider receives the signals sent out by the hand-held transmitter, its electric motors move parts of the aircraft.

RFIDs

Radio Frequency IDentification (RFID) tags either send a radio signal constantly or when scanned. Warehouses and delivery firms use the tags for tracking. They are also fitted to vehicles for toll roads and found in public transport smartcards. In Denmark's Legoland theme park, parents can hire RFID bracelets that track, alert, and locate children who get lost.

→ The Xtag
This electronic ankle tag uses RFID technology. It enables hospital staff to keep track of patients, particularly the young and elderly, who may not be able to say who they are.

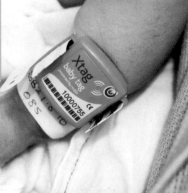

← Taking dictation
The latest speech recognition software can generate almost error-free dictation. It recognizes spoken words and turns them into a text document in real time.

Voice power

Speech is natural, easy for most people to produce, and leaves the hands free for other tasks. The main challenges for voice-controlled technology are cancelling out background noise and recognizing a massive spoken vocabulary. These are being overcome, and voice control is already being used for non-critical functions in vehicles, smartphones, computers, and game play.

↑ Eurofighter Typhoon
Some planes allow a pilot to switch radar mode, control displays, and perform navigation tasks using voice commands.

→ Virtual exploration
A research scientist at the Earth Simulator Center in Yokohama, Japan explores a VR model of the Earth. VR is used in science to study complex structures from any viewpoint or angle.

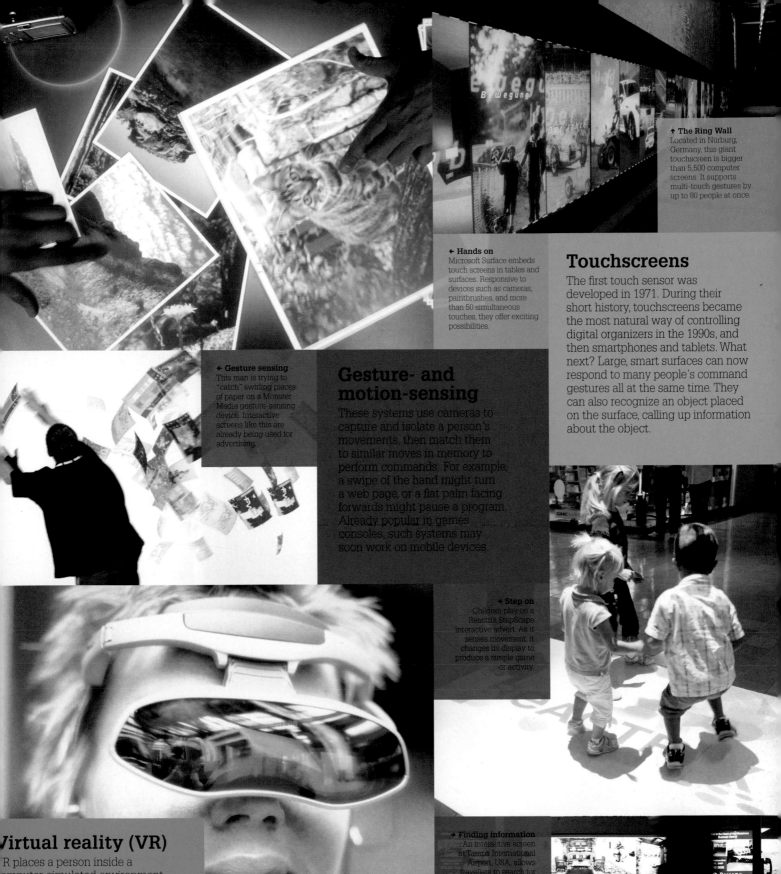

↑ The Ring Wall
Located in Nürburg, Germany, this giant touchscreen is bigger than 5,500 computer screens. It supports multi-touch gestures by up to 80 people at once.

← Hands on
Microsoft Surface embeds touch screens in tables and surfaces. Responsive to devices such as cameras, paintbrushes, and more than 50 simultaneous touches, they offer exciting possibilities.

Touchscreens

The first touch sensor was developed in 1971. During their short history, touchscreens became the most natural way of controlling digital organizers in the 1990s, and then smartphones and tablets. What next? Large, smart surfaces can now respond to many people's command gestures all at the same time. They can also recognize an object placed on the surface, calling up information about the object.

← Gesture sensing
This man is trying to "catch" swirling pieces of paper on a Monster Media gesture-sensing device. Interactive screens like this are already being used for advertising.

Gesture- and motion-sensing

These systems use cameras to capture and isolate a person's movements, then match them to similar moves in memory to perform commands. For example, a swipe of the hand might turn a web page, or a flat palm facing forwards might pause a program. Already popular in games consoles, such systems may soon work on mobile devices.

→ Step on
Children play on a Reactrix StepScape interactive advert. As it senses movement, it changes its display to produce a simple game or activity.

Virtual reality (VR)

VR places a person inside a computer-simulated environment that appears real to the senses. The virtual world is projected inside a head-mounted display (HMD) and interaction is possible via a controller fitted with sensors. VR is used by the military and in industry for teaching, engineering tasks, and testing new product design.

↑ VR glasses
The latest HMDs project fractionally different viewpoints into each eye, which the brain processes into a 3-D view. Sensors track the movement of the head and shift the view.

→ Finding information
An interactive screen at Tampa International Airport, USA, allows travellers to search for accommodation and transport using gestures and a large touchscreen.

Supercomputers

You've been lucky enough to get a pass inside China's National Supercomputing Centre, based in the northern city of Tianjin. Supercomputers are the beasts that governments, universities, and industry use to tackle massive computing tasks. What stands before you, housed in 103 chilled cabinets, is the world's most powerful computer, the Tianhe-1A. It has more processing power than 175,000 top-of-the-range laptop PCs.

Top of the flops

"Flops" (floating-point operations per second) are one way to measure a computer's performance. Home PCs can perform thousands, even millions of flops, but the top supercomputers work in petaflops – a thousand trillion calculations per second! The Tianhe-1A's peak speed is more than 2.5 petaflops.

Did you know?

Computing power increases rapidly each year. The 1970s' supercomputer Cray 1, designed by Seymour Cray (see right), was rated at around 100 megaflops – slower than an Xbox 360 or PS3 games console!

Big beast

The Tianhe-1A contains 14,336 Xeon X5670 processors and 7,168 Nvidia Tesla M2050 graphics cards. It cost around £55 million (US$88 million) to build and a further £12.5 million (US$20 million) a year to run. Its jobs include modelling weather patterns and number-crunching for oil exploration.

What do they do?

Supercomputers are often put to work modelling how galaxies may move and collide (left), how major weather systems form and move, what happens to all the particles in a major explosion, or how atoms behave in a chemical reaction. All these tasks involve mind-numbing amounts of calculation that would take too long on regular computers – or even be impossible to do.

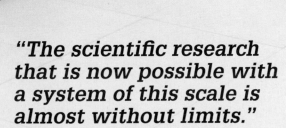

In the past

One man, US electrical engineer Seymour Cray, dominated supercomputer design for decades and continues in the field today. He worked on the world's first commercial supercomputer, 1964's CDC 6600, before forming his own company. Many of Cray's early designs, such as the 1984 X-MP/48 (above), were circular to help reduce the distance that processing signals had to travel.

"The scientific research that is now possible with a system of this scale is almost without limits."

Guangming Liu, chief of the National Supercomputer Centre, China

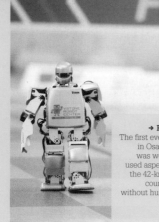

Machine perception

The process of seeing an object, recognizing what it is, and recalling stored information about it – a process called perception – comes naturally to humans. Researchers in the field of machine perception are trying create computers that can do this too. Machines have to use sensors, such as cameras, to "see" their surroundings, and then process and store the data to build up a model of the world.

→ Robot marathon
The first ever robot marathon in Osaka, Japan, in 2011 was won by a robot that used aspects of AI to follow the 42-km- (26-mile-) long course autonomously, without human intervention.

↑ Nexi
The robot *Nexi* is able to view and map the features on a human face to work out what emotion it is showing. Then, in response, it puts a suitable expression on its own face.

Artificial intelligence

American artificial intelligence (AI) pioneer Marvin Minsky described AI as "the science of making machines do things that require intelligence if done by men". That is just one definition. AI draws on many subjects, from computing to psychology. At its cutting edge, it can involve creating machines that can compete with humans.

← Talk of the future
Ray Kurzweil is an inventor and pioneer of many technologies including music synthesizers and machines capable of speech. He believes that further boosts in computing power will lead to major advances in AI.

Intelligent cars

AI research is working towards driverless vehicles (with no human remote control) that can navigate a route, obey traffic rules, and avoid obstacles. The cars must process information from cameras, laser rangefinders, and other instruments. In 2007, the US Department of Defense tested 11 driverless cars over a 96-km (60-mile) course that mimicked city streets. Six reached the end.

The future

Despite AI's frustratingly slow progress, many people remain optimistic about its future. These include the US inventor, author, and lecturer Ray Kurzweil. In 2010, he predicted that "Machines will follow a path that mirrors the evolution of humans. Ultimately, however, self-aware, self-improving machines will evolve beyond humans' ability to control or even understand them."

↑ Boss in action
The winner of the Department of Defense's challenge was a vehicle called *Boss*. The prize was £1.25 million (US$2 million).

Social learning

Researchers are developing machines that learn new tasks and skills by having them work alongside and interact with humans. Robots such as *Leonardo* bring us a step nearer to the goal of a truly intelligent machine. Instead of being programmed for every task, they build up understanding in the same way that humans do – by mimicking the actions and behaviour of other humans.

↑ **Leonardo**
Fitted with a camera, the robot *Leonardo* is capable of recognizing and remembering faces it has seen before. It can also track objects that it is familiar with, moving its head to follow the object's path.

What's on TV?

In 2011, the US trivia quiz show *Jeopardy!* starred its first non-human contestant. The *Watson* program runs on a cluster of fast servers, contains a giant database of facts, and, most importantly, can understand slang and puns. Before buzzing to answer, *Watson* has to narrow down choices, make decisions, and build confidence in its answers by running thousands of checks and comparisons. It may revolutionize machine learning.

↑ **Quiz champion**
In February 2011 on its first network TV appearance, *Watson* defeated two former *Jeopardy!* champions, Brad Rutter and Ken Jennings.

Playing chess

In 2006, Russian Vladimir Kramnik was the chess champion of the world. Then he took on a computer running the *Deep Fritz* chess program and lost 2–4. With its complex moves and strategy, chess has long been used as a test of machine intelligence. IBM's *Deep Blue* chess program, which defeated Russian grand master Garry Kasparov 2–1 in 1996, was able to analyze as many as 200 million different moves.

↑ **Kramnik vs Deep Fritz**
Grand master Vladimir Kramnik considers his next move during his six-game contest against *Deep Fritz*. The chess tournament took place in Bonn, Germany in November 2006.

What makes a robot?

Robots inhabited science fiction films and stories long before they became scientific fact. The first robots emerged in the 1960s and have since exploded in range, size, and versatility. Robots tend to perform human-like actions but with greater precision, repetition, or force than we can ever manage, or in locations we cannot or dare not visit.

Core components

Robots vary greatly in shape, form, and function, but most have similar key parts enabling them to work effectively and efficiently. The vast majority of robots rely on microprocessors and electronics.

Controller

The controller is the processor or "brain" of the robot. It keeps all the parts of the robot working together and makes decisions based on feedback sent to it from the sensors.

Sensors

Devices like touch detectors, GPS, cameras, and temperature sensors send data called feedback back to the controller. These sensors report the robot's condition and position.

End effector

Many robots have parts called end effectors that interact with the environment or manipulate objects. An industrial robot arm, for example, can be fitted with different tools to perform a range of tasks.

Did you know?

The word "robot" comes from the Czech word robota meaning forced labour. It was first used in 1920 in Karel Čapek's play, Rossum's Universal Robots, where human-like machines enslaved people.

What is a robot?

A robot is an automated machine that can be programmed to perform a range of tasks, such as this industrial robot arm playing a game. A robot is able to react to events in its surroundings and make decisions. Some of its parts are capable of movement.

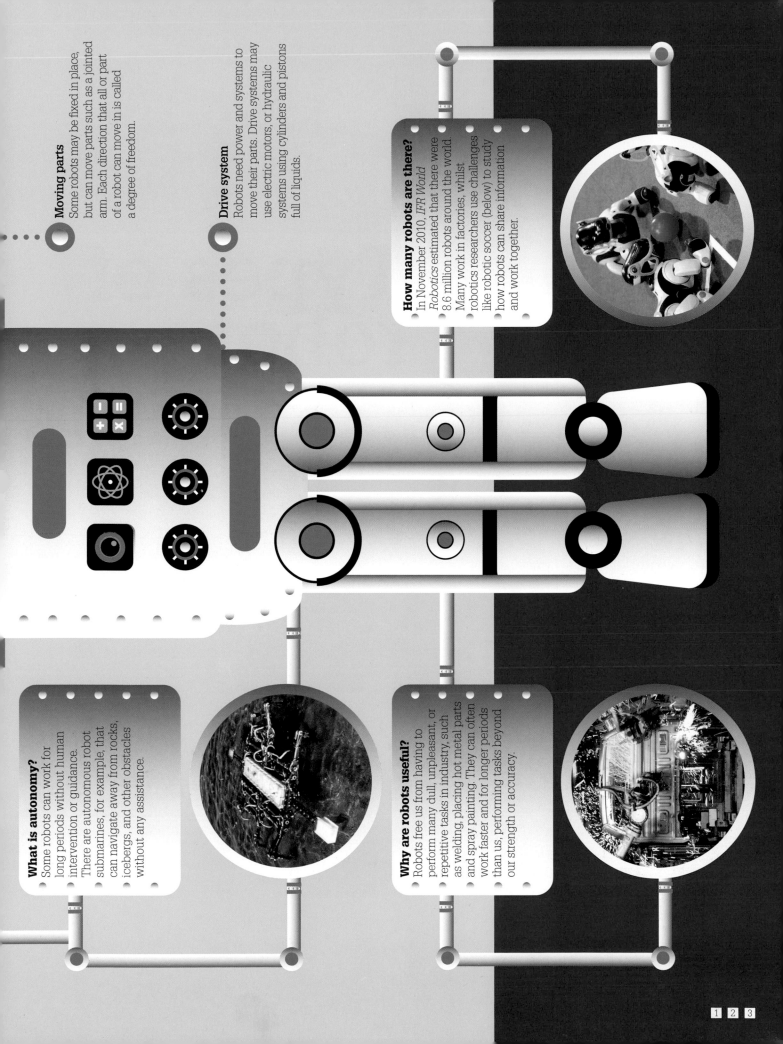

Moving parts

Some robots may be fixed in place, but can move parts such as a jointed arm. Each direction that all or part of a robot can move in is called a degree of freedom.

Drive system

Robots need power and systems to move their parts. Drive systems may use electric motors, or hydraulic systems using cylinders and pistons full of liquids.

How many robots are there?

In November 2010, *IFR World Robotics* estimated that there were 8.6 million robots around the world. Many work in factories, whilst robotics researchers use challenges like robotic soccer (below) to study how robots can share information and work together.

What is autonomy?

Some robots can work for long periods without human intervention or guidance. There are autonomous robot submarines, for example, that can navigate away from rocks, icebergs, and other obstacles without any assistance.

Why are robots useful?

Robots free us from having to perform many dull, unpleasant, or repetitive tasks in industry, such as welding, placing hot metal parts and spray painting. They can often work faster and for longer periods than us, performing tasks beyond our strength or accuracy.

Military robots

In many countries the military has helped to fund robotics research, as well as deploying robots for a range of tasks. In the air, unmanned aerial vehicles (UAVs) are used for surveillance of enemy locations. On the ground, robots patrol military compounds as security guards or move ahead of human troops, finding and disarming unexploded bombs and mines.

→ Robot flyer
This UAV, the MQ-1 Predator, can fly for up to 24 hours at a stretch. Onboard imaging and other surveillance instruments spy on targets on the ground.

→ Bomb disposal
A French military bomb disposal robot approaches an unexploded car bomb. It will blast a jet of water into the bomb to disrupt its circuits.

Types of robot

Robots come in all shapes and sizes, from the tiniest micro aerial vehicles to huge, heavy-lifters used in industry, construction, and space. These hard-working machines perform all sorts of dirty, dangerous, or boring tasks for us. They crawl through sewers, check chemical plants for toxic leaks, defuse bombs – and even flip burgers!

Industrial robots

More than a million robots work in factories around the world. Automated Guided Vehicles (AGVs) transport materials from place to place, while high-speed robot arms work on production lines, assembling, spray-painting, and welding. A small but growing number of robots work in mining, demolition, and other industries.

← Robo dog
In 1999, the Sony AIBO thrilled owners with its ability to respond to speech commands in Spanish or English, take pictures with its cameras, and learn from its environment.

Entertainers and educators

Robots displayed in museums or at events always fascinate and entertain. Building simple robots is a hands-on way to learn about mechanics, electronics, and computing, as well as robotics. With kits such as LEGO Mindstorms™, hobbyists can build, modify, and program their own machines.

↑ Sony QRIO
The singing, dancing QRIO humanoid robot, created in 2003, stood 60 cm (24 in) tall. It had 38 joints and "ran" at 23 cm (9 in) per second – fairly fast for a biped robot.

← Demolition droids
A Brokk demolition robot helps dismantle a nuclear power station laboratory. Demolition robots can operate in high-risk environments, leaving human workers a safe distance away.

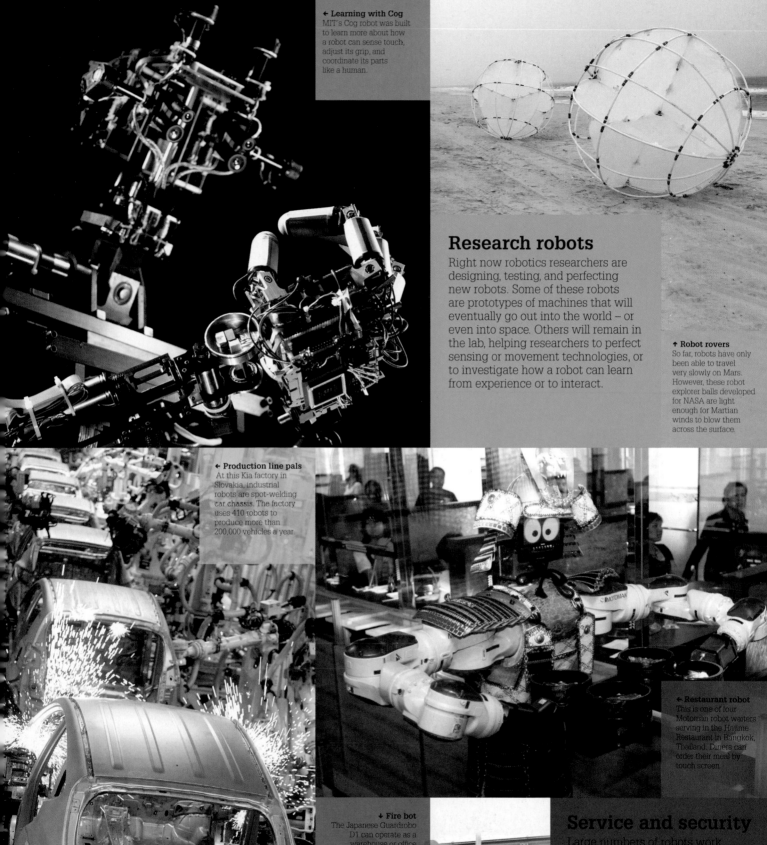

← Learning with Cog
MIT's Cog robot was built to learn more about how a robot can sense touch, adjust its grip, and coordinate its parts like a human.

Research robots

Right now robotics researchers are designing, testing, and perfecting new robots. Some of these robots are prototypes of machines that will eventually go out into the world – or even into space. Others will remain in the lab, helping researchers to perfect sensing or movement technologies, or to investigate how a robot can learn from experience or to interact.

↑ Robot rovers
So far, robots have only been able to travel very slowly on Mars. However, these robot explorer balls developed for NASA are light enough for Martian winds to blow them across the surface.

← Production line pals
At this Kia factory in Slovakia, industrial robots are spot-welding car chassis. The factory uses 410 robots to produce more than 200,000 vehicles a year.

← Restaurant robot
This is one of four Motoman robot waiters serving in the Hajime Restaurant in Bangkok, Thailand. Diners can order their meal by touch screen.

↓ Fire bot
The Japanese Guardrobo D1 can operate as a warehouse or office security guard. It patrols buildings, investigates disturbances, and can detect and extinguish fires.

Service and security

Large numbers of robots work in service industries performing simple, repetitive tasks – cleaning skyscraper windows or airport concourse floors, mowing lawns, or ferrying supplies from place to place. Some even work directly with people as guides, waiters, security guards, and house-sitters.

"Robots have been into the deepest oceans. They've been to Mars. They're just starting to come into your home. You could think of your living room as their Final Frontier."

Cynthia Breazeal

...Star Wars film, Cynthia Breazeal
...fascinated by robotics. The author of
...Sociable Robots, Breazeal is now director
...Group at the MIT (Massachusetts
...of MEDIA LAB. She specializes in
...as Leonardo and Nexi that can interact
...express emotional responses". Kismet
...robot, reacts to human
...expressions with speech,
...of its own.

Did you know?

Breazeal built Leonardo with
help from Stan Winston, the
Oscar-winning special effects
creator behind the monsters
in *Aliens*, *Terminator*,
Predator, *Jurassic Park* and
the Narnia movies.

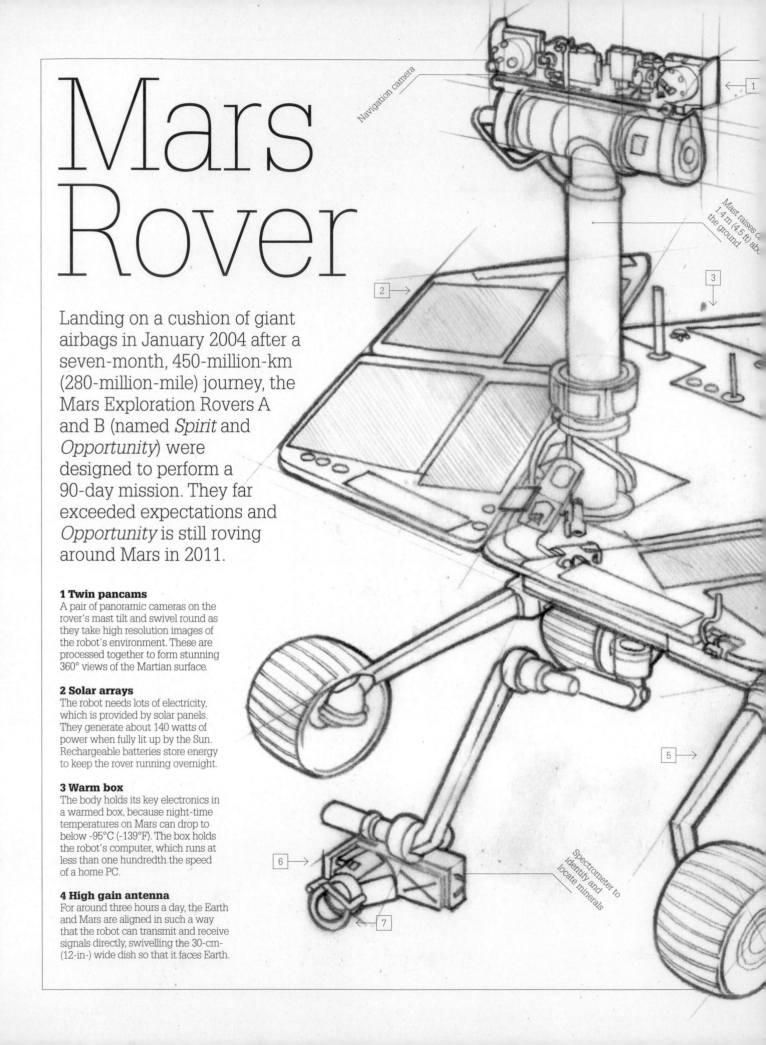

Mars Rover

Landing on a cushion of giant airbags in January 2004 after a seven-month, 450-million-km (280-million-mile) journey, the Mars Exploration Rovers A and B (named *Spirit* and *Opportunity*) were designed to perform a 90-day mission. They far exceeded expectations and *Opportunity* is still roving around Mars in 2011.

1 Twin pancams

A pair of panoramic cameras on the rover's mast tilt and swivel round as they take high resolution images of the robot's environment. These are processed together to form stunning 360° views of the Martian surface.

2 Solar arrays

The robot needs lots of electricity, which is provided by solar panels. They generate about 140 watts of power when fully lit up by the Sun. Rechargeable batteries store energy to keep the rover running overnight.

3 Warm box

The body holds its key electronics in a warmed box, because night-time temperatures on Mars can drop to below -95°C (-139°F). The box holds the robot's computer, which runs at less than one hundredth the speed of a home PC.

4 High gain antenna

For around three hours a day, the Earth and Mars are aligned in such a way that the robot can transmit and receive signals directly, swivelling the 30-cm-(12-in-) wide dish so that it faces Earth.

Navigation camera

Mast raises to 1.4 m (4.5 ft) above the ground

Spectrometer to identify and locate minerals

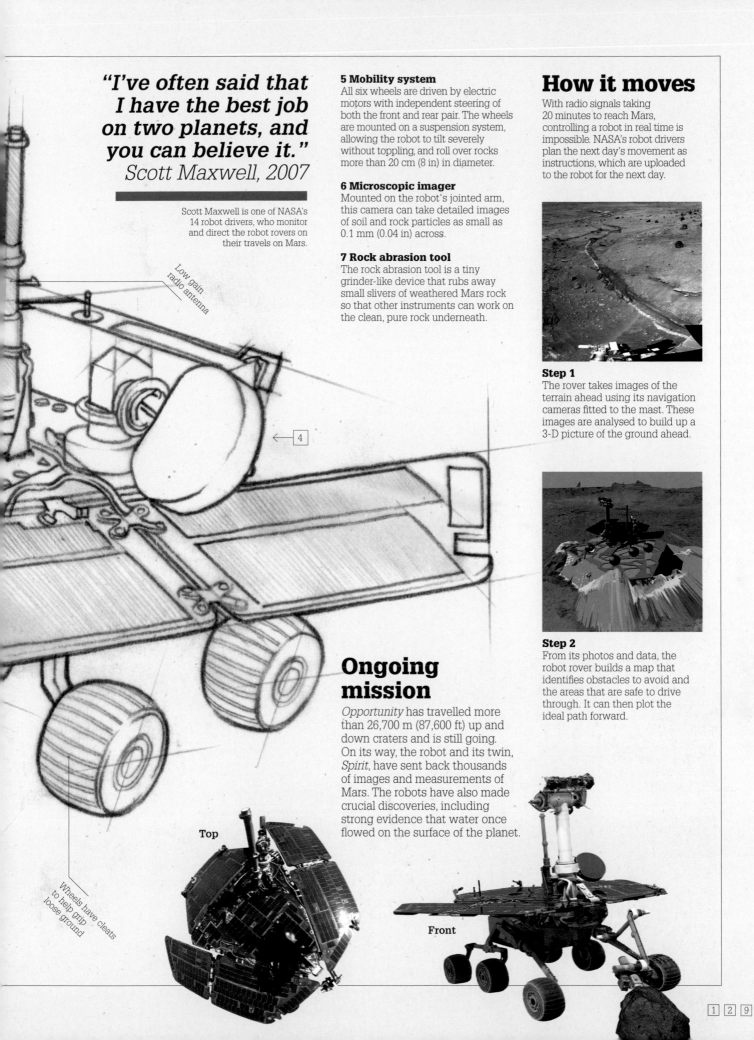

> ## "I've often said that I have the best job on two planets, and you can believe it."
> *Scott Maxwell, 2007*

Scott Maxwell is one of NASA's 14 robot drivers, who monitor and direct the robot rovers on their travels on Mars.

Low gain radio antenna

← 4

Wheels have cleats to help grip loose ground

Top

Front

5 Mobility system
All six wheels are driven by electric motors with independent steering of both the front and rear pair. The wheels are mounted on a suspension system, allowing the robot to tilt severely without toppling, and roll over rocks more than 20 cm (8 in) in diameter.

6 Microscopic imager
Mounted on the robot's jointed arm, this camera can take detailed images of soil and rock particles as small as 0.1 mm (0.04 in) across.

7 Rock abrasion tool
The rock abrasion tool is a tiny grinder-like device that rubs away small slivers of weathered Mars rock so that other instruments can work on the clean, pure rock underneath.

Ongoing mission

Opportunity has travelled more than 26,700 m (87,600 ft) up and down craters and is still going. On its way, the robot and its twin, *Spirit*, have sent back thousands of images and measurements of Mars. The robots have also made crucial discoveries, including strong evidence that water once flowed on the surface of the planet.

How it moves
With radio signals taking 20 minutes to reach Mars, controlling a robot in real time is impossible. NASA's robot drivers plan the next day's movement as instructions, which are uploaded to the robot for the next day.

Step 1
The rover takes images of the terrain ahead using its navigation cameras fitted to the mast. These images are analysed to build up a 3-D picture of the ground ahead.

Step 2
From its photos and data, the robot rover builds a map that identifies obstacles to avoid and the areas that are safe to drive through. It can then plot the ideal path forward.

Robot hospital

Robots are at work in hospitals, performing a surprisingly varied range of tasks. Should you find yourself in hospital at some point in the future, the chances are that some part of your stay will be assisted by robots. They might deliver your meals, prescribe your drugs, or return you to the ward from the operating room. Robots might even perform surgery on you – they are already involved in thousands of operations a year.

Working from the inside

In the future, medical staff may send microscopic robots into patients' bodies, through cavities or tiny incisions. These tiny machines would be able to diagnose problems and fix them from the inside.

● Scientists hope that the microTec submarine (below, imagined inside a human artery), built up from layers of acrylic just 0.001 mm (0.0004 in) thick, might one day travel along blood vessels repairing damage from within.

● In the distant future, even tinier nanorobots, built to the scale of atoms, might be injected into your body to fight diseased cells directly.

Operating theatre
Robots such as the Da Vinci (see right) are becoming a more common sight in the operating theatre. Surgical assistants such as ROBODOC have carried out more than 24,000 knee or hip replacement operations, and can drill, cut, and grip with more accuracy than a human hand. Another robot, Neuromate, can even perform brain surgery.

On the ward
Reducing the workload on porters and nursing staff, automated guided vehicles (AGVs) can fetch and carry blankets, food, and supplies, saving hundreds of working hours. Robots may soon assist with the direct care of patients, lifting people out of bed or alerting human medical staff if a patient falls.

Robotic replacements
Advances in technology are improving the latest generations of replacement body parts, including artificial arms and legs. Packed with microprocessors and sensors, smart prosthetic limbs can adjust the amount of flex or stiffness in the joints, making it easier for the wearer to lift, bend, or walk.

Behind the scenes
Support robots in hospitals do jobs such as clean floors and dispense drugs. The Robot-Rx can handle a dozen prescriptions a minute as it scans bar codes and selects the right drug and dosage from the pharmacy. This robot dispenses some 500 million medications each year in US hospitals.

The HelpMate

Created by Joseph Engelberger (see page 135), HelpMates trundle quietly around hospitals ferrying drugs, blankets, meals, and other essentials. They use light direction and range (LIDAR) scanners to track light, determine direction, and work out their distance from obstacles.

CareBot and NurseBot

Researchers are working on prototype personal robotic companions to help care for the elderly. CareBot (left) and NurseBot could help patients with exercises, remind them to take medicine, raise the alarm in an emergency, and act as a link to the outside world.

The DEKA Arm

Advanced prosthetic limbs can give an amputee almost the same range of movement as a human arm. The DEKA weighs around 3.6 kg (8 lb) – about the same as a woman's arm. It contains numerous microprocessors and compact electric motors to control movement.

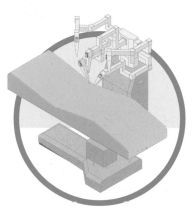

Da Vinci

Providing 3-D images from inside the body, this multi-armed robot works with pinpoint precision under the control of a human surgeon. More than 1,500 hospitals worldwide have one or more da Vincis, and these robots perform hundreds of thousands of operations a year.

MySpoon

Designed by SECOM in Japan, the award-winning MySpoon arm helps the ill, disabled, or elderly at meal times by scooping up manageable portions of food and raising them to the person's mouth. Operated by a single push button, it can handle any food – from soup to spaghetti.

First responders

Rescue robots can help at the scene of a disaster or accident. They can clamber over or through rubble to find victims, using thermal-imaging cameras, and make contact with rescuers. They can also deliver lifesaving oxygen, water, or medicine.

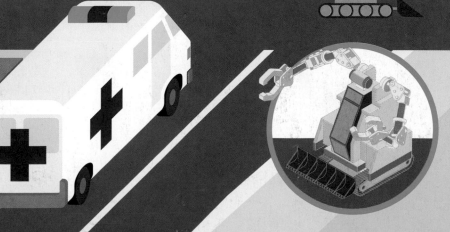

Tmsuk Enryu

This powerful Japanese "rescue dragon" robot stands 3.5 m (11.5 ft) tall and can tear off car doors so that medical staff can reach victims trapped inside. Each of its twin robot arms is able to lift up to 500 kg (1,100 lb), making them strong enough to carry people to safety.

Space

Airless, waterless, freezing-cold space is the ultimate challenge for exploration. Robots are usually sent on one-way missions, never to return, but the results of their work – thousands of photographs and scientific readings – can be beamed back to Earth.

Robot explorers

Robots can make excellent explorers. They do not need the oxygen, water, and food that human explorers demand. Instead, they use batteries or fuel cells, or even generate their own energy from solar panels. Robots can also be sent on high-risk journeys with little or no hope of return. The toughest ones are built to withstand extremes, from the pressures of the ocean depths tc the temperatures in space, which average a bitter -255 °C (-427 °F) but can reach hundreds of degrees.

Sky

Flying robots have many uses. They are used to explore and map isolated areas, from remote forests to icy wastes, and also to spy on enemy territory. The *Robofalcon* has a less impressive but no less important job – scaring away bird flocks from airport runways.

Viking landers

In July 1976, after a 10-month journey through space, *Viking 1* landed on Mars. It was followed, about 6 weeks later, by *Viking 2*. The robots took the first colour images of the planet's surface. Their arms picked up and analysed soil samples, and then radioed the results back to Earth.

Voyager 1

Launched in 1977, this long-distance space probe is still sending back data. *Voyager 1* is now in the outer reaches of the Solar System after a 22-billion-km (13-billion-mile) journey past Jupiter, Saturn, Uranus, and Neptune.

Canadarm2

Astronauts can ride on this giant robot arm attached to the International Space Station, in orbit 350 km (220 miles) above the Earth. *Canadarm2* is 17.6 m (57.7 ft) long and can handle payloads weighing up to 116,000 kg (226,000 lb).

QinetiQ Zephyr

This solar-powered robot with a 22.5-m (74-ft) wingspan is designed to fly slowly, but for long periods, carrying out aerial photography or surveillance at low cost. In July 2010, it flew non-stop for a staggering 14 days and 21 minutes.

Micro Aerial Vehicles (MAVs)

Still under development, MAVs are robot fliers, often no bigger than your hand, intended for local exploration, aerial photography, and police surveillance. One day, squadrons of MAVs may fly search-and-rescue missions.

Global Hawk

This military Unmanned Aerial Vehicle (UAV) has a 35.4-m (116-ft) wingspan and is used to explore large areas of terrain in a single flight. Its onboard surveillance equipment includes high-resolution cameras and radar.

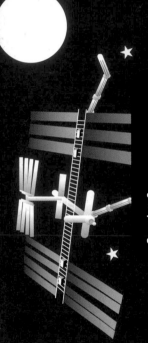

Land

Land robots have crossed deserts, found meteorites in Antarctica, and inched into the mouths of active volcanoes. Other land explorers may not make the news but still perform vital work such as seeking out cracks or leaks in pipelines.

Pyramid explorer

In 2002, iRobot Pyramid Rover entered the heart of the Great Pyramid at Giza, Egypt, through a 20-cm (8-in) wide shaft.

• The rover travelled 64 m (210 ft) along the shaft to find its way blocked by a stone.

• The robot drilled a hole through the stone and then fed in a small, fibre-optic camera to view inside the chamber.

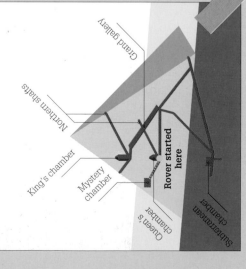

Grand gallery

Northern shafts

King's chamber

Mystery chamber

Queen's chamber

Subterranean chamber

Rover started here

Mobile robot swarm

In the future, swarms of small, simple land robots may be used to search an area quickly but effectively for a missing person or object. Robots like this could be equipped with tracks or with jointed legs for climbing over rough terrain.

Pyramid explorers

Small robots may unlock the mysteries that lie inside the 4,600-year-old Great Pyramid in Giza, Egypt. Just 12 cm (4.7 in) tall and 5 cm (1.9 in) wide, iRobot's rover has tracks on its top and bottom for gripping the floor or roof.

Autosubs under Antartica

The hostile waters around Antarctica claimed the *Autosub 2* robot in 2005. Four years later, *Autosub 3*, powered by 5,000 D-cell torch batteries, dived beneath 500 m (1,640 ft) of solid ice to explore the floating polar ice shelves.

Nereus

Powered by 2,000 lithium-ion batteries, *Nereus* is a 4.25-m- (14-ft-) long robot sub. In 2009, it explored the Pacific's Challenger Deep trench, a depth of 10,902 m (35,768 ft). Only one robot, *Kaiko* (see page 135), has dived deeper.

Sea

Study underwater robots are sometimes used on journeys to the seabed that might prove deadly to human divers. They are sent to salvage key parts of downed aircraft or ancient shipwrecks, or to study underwater life or geology.

Advance of the robot

It all started with a squat box with an extended, jointed arm that ▮▮led red-hot metal castings in a car factory. Deployed in 1961, the Unimate was the world's first industrial robot, capable of learning 200 commands. Before then, gifted mechanical engineers had assembled machines that performed automated tasks... but nothing that matched the versatility of a true robot. Robotics is still in its infancy, but here are some of the milestones that have made it such an exciting field of research.

Did you know?

In 2003, an Odyssey Marine Exploration underwater robot, *ZEUS*, helped recover more than 51,000 gold and silver coins from the 1865 shipwreck of the SS *Republic*.

↘ 1801
Joseph-Marie Jacquard invents the first programmable machine – a weaving loom where the patterns are controlled by a series of cards with holes punched in them.

↑ 1948
Professor Norbert Weiner of Massachusetts Institute of Technology (MIT), USA, publishes his influential book, *Cybernetics*. It looks at how communications and control work in animals, and how they might work in machines.

↓ 1970–3
A team at Waseda University, Japan, build *Wabot-1*, the first life-size humanoid robot. It has a pair of arms and legs, two cameras for simple eyes, but no head.

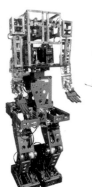

1984
The humanoid robot *Wabot-2* is built at Waseda University. It reads sheet music through its camera eye and plays the organ with its 10 fingers and two feet.

↑ 1966
At the Stanford Research Institute, work begins on *Shakey*, the first autonomous moving robot able to navigate around obstacles. Its top speed is 2 m (6.5 ft) per hour.

↑ 1976
The *Viking 1* and *2* spacecraft land on Mars. Their robot arms are the first robots to reach another planet.

c. 270 BCE
Greek scholar Ctesibius of Alexandria designs pumps and water clocks with complex mechanisms.

1938
The first programmable spray-painting machine is designed for the DeVilbiss Company.

1956
Joe Engelberger and George Devol form the world's first robotics company, Unimation.

1981
Japanese scientist Takeo Kanade builds the first direct-drive robot arm, installing electric motors directly into the joints of the arm to make its movements faster and more accurate.

↓ 1738
French inventor Jacques de Vaucanson creates a mechanical duck that can mimic some of the actions of a real one.

1920
Czech playwright Karel Capek coins the term "robot" in his play *Rossum's Universal Robots*.

1959
The Artificial Intelligence Laboratory at MIT is founded.

1986
The Remotely Operated Vehicle (ROV) *Jason Junior* photographs the *Titanic* shipwreck on the Atlantic Ocean floor.

↑ 1942
Isaac Asimov writes a story about robots, *Runaround*, which contains his Three Laws of Robotics. He later adds a Zeroth Law. These laws have influenced robot development in real life as well as in books and movies.

1961
In the USA, the first Unimate robot begins work in the Trenton, New Jersey, General Motors factory. It puts in a 100,000-hour shift before retiring and going on display at the Smithsonian Museum.

↑ 1970
The Soviet Union's *Lunokhod 1* moon rover becomes the first machine to move across the surface of a body other than Earth. The eight-wheeled rover travels more than 10 km (6 miles).

↑ 1975
The PUMA (Programmable Universal Machine for Assembly) industrial robot arm is invented.

↑ 1979
The Stanford Cart autonomous robotic vehicle navigates a room of obstacles.

Joseph F Engelberger

Inspired by the sci-fi *I, Robot* stories of Isaac Asimov, Engelberger joined up with engineer George Devol to form the world's first robotics company, Unimation, in 1956. Their robots inspired companies in Japan, Korea, and northern Europe. In the mid-1980s, Engelberger moved into service robots, producing a series of HelpMate robots for hospitals. Now in his eighties, Engelberger still lectures and writes on robotics.

"Robot builders today have more technology available to them than has ever been used."

Joe Engelberger, 2003, in an interview with Bloomberg Businessweek

↑ 1989
The first HelpMate Automated Guided Vehicle (AGV) starts work ferrying supplies around a US hospital.

↓ 1997
Sojourner is the first robot to move around the surface of another planet, Mars.

↖ 2001
The Unmanned Aerial Vehicle (UAV) *Global Hawk* makes the first autonomous non-stop flight over the Pacific Ocean. The journey from California, USA, to southern Australia takes 22 hours.

2001
A ZEUS surgery robot performs a gall bladder operation on a patient in France, controlled by Dr Jacques Marescaux, a surgeon in New York.

2010
A da Vinci robotic surgeon and a robotic anaesthetist, *McSleepy*, perform the first all-robot surgery on a patient in Canada.

↓ 2010
Robonaut 2 becomes the first humanoid robot in space when it rides on the *Discovery* space shuttle to the International Space Station. Future robonauts will be able to perform space walks, repair spacecraft and probes, and may even explore planets.

↑ 2005
The Robosapien V2 toy is launched.

1995
The *Kaiko* ROV reaches the deepest part of the Pacific Ocean, 10,911 m (35,797 ft) below sea level.

2004
The Mars Exploration Rovers *Spirit* and *Opportunity* touch down on Mars and begin to rove across its surface.

2008
The number of industrial robots tops one million for the first time. More than a third work in factories in Japan.

1990
The ROBODOC surgical assistant robot is invented and trialled, helping to perform a hip replacement operation on a dog. Two years later, it operates on its first human patient.

1994
Marc Thorpe begins the combat robot competition, *Robot Wars*, in the USA.

1994
The eight-legged *Dante II* robot samples gases inside the Mount Spurr volcano in Alaska, USA.

1998
LEGO releases its first programmable Robotics Invention System (RIS) bricks, *Mindstorms*.

↓ 1999
Sony's AIBO (Artificial Intelligence roBOt) dog goes on sale.

2002
A Predator UAV attacks an al-Qaeda terrorist convoy in Afghanistan, the first known deliberate attack on humans using robots.

→ 2007
Honda's latest ASIMO humanoid robot is unveiled, boasting a top running speed of 6 kph (3.7 mph).

↓ 2009
More than three million iRobot Roomba vacuuming robots have been sold worldwide, making it the bestselling consumer robot of all time.

← 1998
Work begins at MIT on *Kismet*, which reacts to its environment and conveys emotions through facial expressions.

→ 2002
Humanoid robots play football at RoboCup for the first time.

> *"There is no reason anyone would want a computer in their home."*
>
> **Ken Olsen**, co-founder and CEO of Digital Equipment Corp. (DEC), 1977

Future promise

Scientists, businesspeople, and writers of the past promised us a future world of personal jet packs, frequent space travel, and cities in the sky. Technology has not delivered on these things yet. What people underestimated, though, was the rise of computing and the Internet.

What next?

The worlds of computing, gadgets, gaming, and the Internet are constantly evolving. Some developments, such as personal robots or videophones, have been a long time coming. Others, such as the booming World Wide Web, were more sudden and took people by surprise. Predictions are always risky, but some key players have been confident enough to suggest what might be in store in both the near and more distant future.

> *"In 30 years, chores around the house will be a thing of the past. The robots will have evolved from automatic appliances to home automations systems."*
>
> **Helen Greiner**, co-founder of iRobot and The Droid Works robotics companies, 2009

The pace of evolution

The speed of change is accelerating. It took thousands of years of human development before the invention of printing made it possible to spread knowledge widely, but less than 50 years to go from the first ever computers to the World Wide Web. Today, with a worldwide Internet-linked audience keen to adopt and adapt to new technologies, it is likely that change will happen even faster.

> *"They say a year in the Internet business is like a dog year… equivalent to 7 years in a regular person's life. In other words, it's evolving faster and faster."*
>
> **Vinton Cerf**, Internet pioneer and, since 2005, a vice president of Google

Thought control

One day you may be able to control gadgets and programs using only your brain and thought patterns. The field is in its infancy, but research is ongoing at many universities and at military and medical organizations. Several have already built headsets that measure brain activity and convert it into commands for appliances and games.

Nanotechnology

Robots and machines built at "nano" scale are measured in nanometres, or millionths of millimetres. If nanotechnology becomes cheap and abundant enough, its impact could be enormous. Thousands of microscopic nanorobots could be sent to work inside machines and human bodies to repair any damage, whilst entire computer systems could be built on a pinhead.

Smartware

Software is only going to get smarter and more personal, able to tailor itself to people's individual requirements and freeing them from a range of mundane tasks. Homes and domestic appliances are likely to be controllable over the Internet. Electrical power supply, too, is going wireless. This smart kitchen counter powers blenders, toasters, and special pans by placing them on the counter's "hotspots".

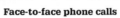

Face-to-face phone calls

Video calls were often predicted or promised in the past but always led to disappointment. They are finally a reality. Apple's FaceTime is just the start. New-generation smartphones and tablets use cameras to stream live images over an Internet connection to enable face-to-face conversations. As the price of making such calls drops, new social networking sites based on real-time video links may boom.

3-D printers

Printers that can output 3-D objects are already here. They take thin, cross-section "slices" of a 3-D computer file and then print the slices. An additive material, such as melted nylon powder, builds up the 3-D object, layer upon layer. In the future, this amazing technology might make it possible to generate processors, entire circuit boards, and spare parts at home.

The future of gaming

Gaming is likely to become even more diverse, with motion-sensing activities for casual gamers and increasingly immersive game worlds for dedicated gamers. Non-player characters equipped with AI will help populate virtual worlds and offer richer gaming experiences. Back in the real world, games competitions on TV may make celebrities of the world's leading players.

Always-on networking

The future of Internet connectivity is all about more – more speed, power, and bandwidth, more availability, and more apps taking advantage of always-on Internet access. Increasing numbers of people will get Internet access. And as more become reliant on the Internet for work, education, information, and play, the pressures on its routers, servers, cabling, and management will grow.

"The future is really terrific and software is a big part of it... I am very optimistic we are really at a tipping point of some great stuff."

Nolan Bushnell, Atari co-founder, 2010

Glossary

ARPANET

A pioneering computer network, founded in 1969, and considered the forerunner of the Internet. It was funded by the USA's Advanced Research Project Agency (ARPA).

Artificial Intelligence (AI)

The intelligence of machines. Also, the science and study of building machines that can learn and think in human-like ways.

authentication

The process of checking the identity of a user, program, or computer on the Web.

avatar

A graphic figure that represents you on messageboards, in chat rooms, and in 3-D virtual worlds.

bandwidth (computing)

The maximum amount of data that can travel along a communications path, such as a cable, in a set time. It is often measured in kilobits or megabits per second.

Bluetooth

A wireless system that uses radio waves to transmit data over short distances. It is used to allow communication between a mobile phone and its hands-free set, for example.

broadband

Telecommunications systems where a single cable can transmit a number of channels of data all at the same time and at high speed.

browser

A computer program that allows people to find, view and navigate between different websites or web pages.

client

A computer that accesses a service or data on another computer via a network.

e-book

A digital version of a printed book available in a file that can be sent via a network and read on a computer or e-reader device.

fibre-optic cable

Cable made of thin strands of glass (or other transparent materials) that carries data over great distances in the form of pulses of light.

game engine

A software system designed to build and run video games. Its tasks include creating graphics and moving objects in the game.

gigabyte (GB)

1,000 megabytes. Hard disk drives are usually measured in GB capacity.

GPS

Short for Global Positioning System, a means of navigation that uses a series of satellites orbiting Earth to give an accurate position on the Earth's surface.

graphical user interface (GUI)

A system that lets users interact with their computer via small images called icons and a cursor pointer, instead of typing in text.

HTML

Short for hypertext markup language, a basic computer language used to format and provide links on text-based web pages.

humanoid (robotics)

A robot that has human features, either in its appearance or its actions.

hyperlink

A word, phrase, image, or icon on the World Wide Web that, if clicked, takes the user to a new document or web page.

Internet

A global network made up of many networks, through which computers communicate by sending data in small units called packets. Each network consists of computers connected by cables or wireless links. The World Wide Web is accessed by means of the Internet.

Local Area Network (LAN)

A network in which computers and other devices are connected together within a small physical area using cables or wireless links.

mainframe

A large, powerful computer, often serving many connected terminals, and usually used by large, complex organizations.

malware

Malicious software that can be transmitted to others by email or downloads.

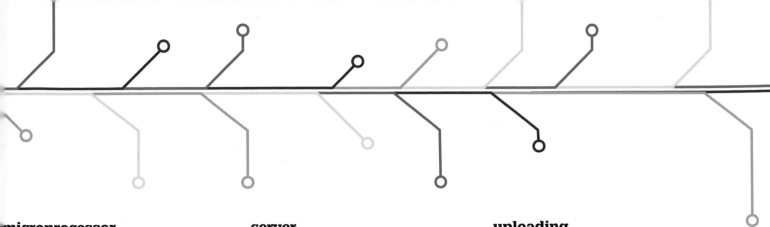

microprocessor

A computer chip that contains most or all of the central processing unit (CPU) of a computer.

MIT

The Massachusetts Institute of Technology, a leading centre of computing, technology, and robotics research in the USA.

nanotechnology

The science of building machines in sizes measured in nanometres. A nanometre is a millionth of a millimetre (0.00000004 in).

open-source software

Free software that can be modified by advanced users for their own purposes.

operating system

The program that manages a computer's resources. Its tasks include sending data to a screen and organizing files.

pixel

Short for "picture element", a pixel is a tiny dot of light on a screen that together with thousands more make up the images on a display.

random access memory (RAM)

Memory used by a computer to hold data that is currently in use and to perform operations on it. Data stored in RAM is usually lost when the machine is turned off.

router

A device that routes data between different networks either via cables or wirelessly.

sensor

A device that gives a robot or computer data about itself or its environment, such as temperature or location.

server

A computer, or software on a computer, that provides services to other computers that connect to it via a network.

SLR

Short for "single lens reflex", a type of camera where the user views the scene to be photographed through the lens of the camera. SLRs can be fitted with a range of lenses and can produce very high quality images.

sonar

A system that uses pulses of sound waves to detect solid objects or to measure distances.

streaming

The ability to send music or video over the Internet as a continuous stream of data so that users can view or listen to it in real time, without waiting to download a complete file.

tablet

A type of computing device that uses a touchscreen for input as well as display.

TCP/IP

Short for "transmission control protocol/ Internet protocol", a set of communications rules that control how data is transferred between computers on the Internet.

torrent file

A way of greater sharing online where parts of the file are downloaded from a number of servers. Each downloading user becomes a source for others who want the same file.

touchscreen

An electronic device that responds to the touch of fingers or a stylus and can be used to input data or select options.

uploading

The process of transferring data from one computer to another or from a storage device to a computer.

virtual reality (VR)

A simulated, interactive 3-D environment, displayed in real time, used for education, entertainment, and in product design.

virus

A program that is capable of duplicating itself and infecting computers. Viruses vary from harmless nuisances to major security risks that can cripple computer systems.

website

A group of related web pages that give information about a particular subject, company, or institution.

Wide Area Network (WAN)

Computer networks that are connected together over long distances using telephone lines, fibre-optic cables, or satellite links.

Wi-Fi

The technology that allows computers and other devices to communicate with each other using wireless signals.

World Wide Web (WWW)

An interconnected set of hypertext documents spread throughout the Internet. The documents are formatted in HTML and kept on computers called servers.

Index

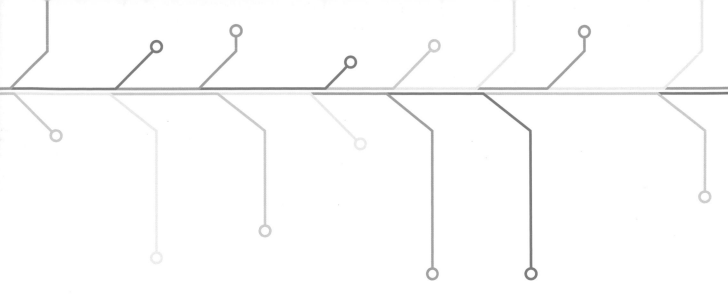

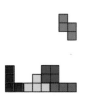

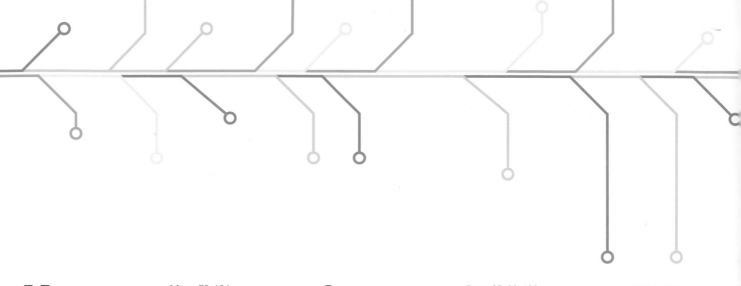

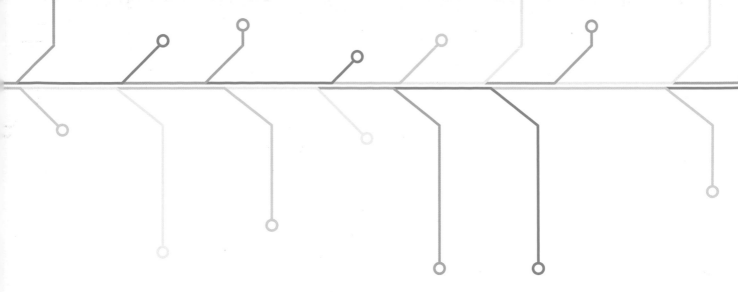

Credits

DK would like to thank:
Stefan Podhorodecki and June Chanpoomidole for help with design. Carron Brown, Victoria Hayworth-Dunne, and Jonathan Garbett for editorial help. Charlotte Webb for proofreading. John Searcy for Americanization. Jackie Brind for the index. Stefan Podhorodecki and Robert Scoble for photography. Roland Smithies for additional picture research.

The author would like to thank:
Steve Mersereau of Red Ink.

The publisher would like to thank the following for their kind permission to reproduce their photographs:
(Key: a–above; b–below/bottom; c–centre; l–left; r–right; t–top. Where there are many images, they are also labelled alphabetically, from left to right from top to bottom.)

8 **Corbis:** Bettmann (cl). **8–9 Corbis:** Bettmann (c). **9 Getty Images:** Hulton Archive (tc). **Science Photo Library:** Nelson Morris (bc). **12 Computer History Museum:** Mark Richards (g). **Corbis:** Kim Kulish (h); Tetra Images (a). **Getty Images:** SSPL (c, d, f); The Bridgeman Art Library (b). **Image originally created by IBM Corporation:** (i). **Photolibrary:** Fotosearch Value (e). **13 Alamy Images:** imagebroker (e); John Joannides (k). **Associated Press AP:** Marcio Jose Sanchez (tl). **Computer History Museum:** (b); Mark Richards (i). © **Intel Corporation:** (c). **Getty Images:** Phil Matt / Liaison (g); SSPL (d, f, j). **Getty Images:** Apic (c). **14 SRI International:** (cl). **15 Getty Images:** Hulton Archive (ca). **SRI International:** (tc, tr, br). **Getty Images:** SSPL (tc). **Science Photo Library:** Martin Dohrn (cl). **16–17 Corbis:** D&P Valenti / ClassicStock (c). **Getty Images:** SSPL (br). **17 Getty Images:** Ted Foxx (tr). **Corbis:** Lawrence Manning (br). **Getty Images:** Scott Davis / Department Of Defense (DOD) / Time Life Pictures (crb). **18 Acer:** (tl). **19 Corbis:** Tim Pannell (br); Terry Why / Monsoon / Photolibrary (cr). **20–21 Corbis:** Ed Quinn. **20 Robert Scoble :** (cra). **21 Corbis:** Pallava Bagla (cr). **NCSA/University of Illinois:** (tl). **24–25 Getty Images:** David Clapp / Oxford Scientific (c). **25 Alamy Images:** Ron Niebrugge (tr). **www.subcom.com:** (cb). **27 Terremark Worldwide, Inc. 28 Alamy Images:** SiliconValleyStock (tr). **Corbis:** Wu Kaixiang / Xinhua Press; Richard Nowitz / National Geographic Society (tl). **Getty Images:** Panoramic Images (b). **29 Alamy Images:** MTP (tr); TJP (clb). **Corbis:** Kim Kulish (cla). **Getty Images:** Ryan Anson / Bloomberg (cb); Gabriel Bouys / AFP (tl); Randi Lynn Beach / Bloomberg (bl); Tony Avelar / Bloomberg (br). **Symantec Corporation:** (cra). **32–33 Courtesy of Apple. 33 Corbis:** Bettmann (cl). **34–35 Corbis:** Terry W. Eggers. **36 Baidu Image Search Service:** (ca). **36–37 Seznam. cz, a.s. :** (tc). **37 Corbis:** Peter Foley / Epa (tr). **38–39**

Corbis: Catherine Karnow (c). © **Google Inc. Used with permission:** (Google icons and logos). **38 Corbis:** Penni Gladstone / San Francisco Chronicle (bc). **39 Corbis:** Mario Anzuoni / Reuters (crb). **Getty Images:** Justin Sullivan (tc). **40–41 Bahnhof AB. 50 Getty Images:** Prakash Mathema / AFP (cb). **50–51 Getty Images:** Prakash Mathema / AFP. **51 Getty Images:** Prakash Mathema / AFP (tc). **Ncell :** (tr). **53 Corbis:** Ding Xiaochun / XinHua / Xinhua Press (tc). **61 Alamy Images:** Gary Lucken. **64 Corbis:** Nasa / Reuters (bl). **71 Getty Images:** Barcroft Media (crb); **Science Photo Library:** Bernhard Edmaier (cra). **72–73** © **Google Inc. Used with permission:** Google Earth. **76 Corbis:** Justin Lane (h); Louie Psihoyos (c). **Fotolia:** ErickN (g); Julián Rovagnati (e); Seth (d). **Image originally created by IBM Corporation:** (f). **Twitter:** (e). **77 Adobe Systems Incorporated:** (c). **Amazon.com, Inc:** (f). **Courtesy of Apple:** (i). **Fotolia:** vectorsmartini (k). **Used with permission from Microsoft:** (g). **Mozilla:** (d). **Napster LLC:** (h). **youtube.com:** (j). **78 Alamy Images:** Art Directors & TRIP (bl). **Corbis:** Maurice Ambler / Hulton Archive (tr). **Qidenus Technologies Gmbh:** (tr). **79 Alamy Images:** Asia Photopress (bl). **Corbis:** H. Armstrong Roberts (tr). **Getty Images:** Saul Loeb / AFP (br); Michael Ochs Archives (tl); Justin Sullivan (bl). **82–83 Corbis:** Atlantide Phototravel. **83 Getty Images:** Anne Frank Fonds / Anne Frank House (bl). © **Google Inc. Used with permission:** (c). **Science Photo Library:** Sam Ogden (tc). **84 Scott Beale / Laughing Squid:** (bl). **84–85 Corbis:** Roger Ressmeyer (bc). **85 Alamy Images:** Wendy White (tl). **Getty Images:** SSPL (cra, bc). **85 Alamy Images:** ArcadeImages. **86 Corbis:** Bettmann (cl). **87 Corbis:** HO / Reuters (tc). **90–91 Corbis:** Fred Prouser / Reuters. **Nintendo:** (tc). **90 Getty Images:** ICHIRO / Photodisc (l). **Nintendo:** (c, crb). **91 Nintendo:** (cb). **93 Alamy Images:** Arterra Picture Library (tr). **94 Used with permission from Microsoft:** (tr). **103 Used with permission from Microsoft:** (ftr). **Nintendo:** (tr). **Sony Computer Entertainment America:** (tc). **106 Alamy Images:** ArcadeImages (br); Sinibomb Images (cla). **Dorling Kindersley:** (fcrb). **Lebrecht Music and Arts:** Interfoto (cl, bl). **Rex Features:** Peter Brooker (bc). **Wikipedia, The Free Encyclopedia:** (cr); Evan Amos (fbr). Moviestore Collection Ltd (fcl); Hugh Threlfall (cr); Finnbarr Webster (clb); toy Alan King (cb); Tony Cordoza (crb); Lightly Salted (br). **Getty Images:** Urbano Delvalle (c); Albert L Ortega (tl); Hulton Archive (br); Jordan Strauss (fcr). **110–111 Corbis:** Frans Lanting. **110 Photolibrary:** (bl). **SanDisk Corporation:** (cl). **114–115 Corbis:** Ocean. **114 Corbis:** Kim Kyung-Hoon / Reuters (c). **115 Corbis:** Benelux (tr); Bill Ross (cb). **116 Alamy Images:** Roderick Smith (crb). **Getty Images:** Ghislain & Marie David de Lossy (tl); Kent Smith /

First Light (clb); Yoshikazu Tsuno / AFP (br). **Rex Features:** Action Press (bc). **WowWee Group Limited:** (tr). **117 Corbis:** Ausloeser (bl); Robert Sorbo / Reuters (tl); Rick Wilking / Reuters (cla); Najlah Feanny (crb); Mcintyre, Scott / ZUMA Press (br). **SENSORY-MINDS GMBH:** (tr). **118–119 Corbis:** Imaginechina. **119 Science Photo Library:** David Parker (br); Daniel Price (tc). **120 Corbis:** Ed Murray / Star Ledger (clb). **Getty Images:** Yoshikazu Tsuno / AFP (tr). **MIT Media Lab :** (tl). **Used with permission, GM Media Archives.:** Jason Cohn / Carnegie Mellon Tartan Racing (br). **121 Corbis:** Ina Fassbender / X00970 / Reuters (b). **Getty Images:** Ben Hider (tr). **Science Photo Library:** Sam Ogden (tl). **122 Getty Images:** Philippe Lopez / AFP (bc). **123 Corbis:** Car Culture (br). **Getty Images:** Yoshikazu Tsuno / AFP (tr). **Science Photo Library:** Peter Menzel (bl). **124 Associated Press AP:** USAF (tr). **Getty Images:** Yuriko Nakao / Reuters (bc). **Dounreay Site Restoration Ltd:** (br). **Science Photo Library:** Pascal Goetgheluck (cla). **125 Corbis:** Narong Sangnak / Epa (crb). **Department of Mechanical and Aerospace Engineering at North Carolina State University:** **Reuters:** Issei Kato IK / TY (bc); Radovan Stoklasa (bl). **Science Photo Library:** Sam Ogden (tl). **129 NASA:** JPL; JPL / Cornell University / Maas Digital (br); JPL-Caltech / Cornell (bc). **Science Photo Library:** NASA / JPL-CALTECH / CORNELL (cra). **130 Science Photo Library:** Eye Of Science (bl). **134 akg-images:** RIA Nowost (h). **The Bridgeman Art Library:** CNAM, Conservatoire National des Arts et Metiers, Paris / Giraudon (a). **Computer History Museum:** (i, j); Mark Richards (c). **Corbis:** Bettmann (f); Lowell Georgia (g). **Science Photo Library:** Peter Menzel (d). **135 Cody Images:** (c). **Corbis:** Gary I Rothstein / Epa (e); Toshiyuki Aizawa / Reuters (i). **Getty Images:** (g); SSPL (b). **iRobot Corporation:** (j). **Rex Features:** (d); Everett Collection (tl); Times Newspapers Ltd (a). **Science Photo Library:** Mauro Fermariello (f); Peter Menzel (f). **136 Corbis:** Stoyan Nenov / X01507 (cb). **Getty Images:** Time & Life Pictures (tc). **iRobot Corporation:** (cra). **Science Photo Library:** Volker Steger (bc); Victor Habbick Visions (br). **137 Alamy Images:** Emmanuel Lattes (cra). **Corbis:** Heide Benser (tr). **Getty Images:** Robyn Beck / AFP (tl); Kevin Winter (bc). **Science Photo Library:** Studio Macbeth

Front jacket: Alamy / Hugh Threlfall (tl); Sony Computer Entertainment (tr); **Corbis / Road and Track / Transtock** (br); ICHIRO / Getty Images (br); **Fotolia / jirkacafa** (bl); **Fotolia / sharpnose** (bl)

All other images © Dorling Kindersley
For further information see: www.dkimages.com

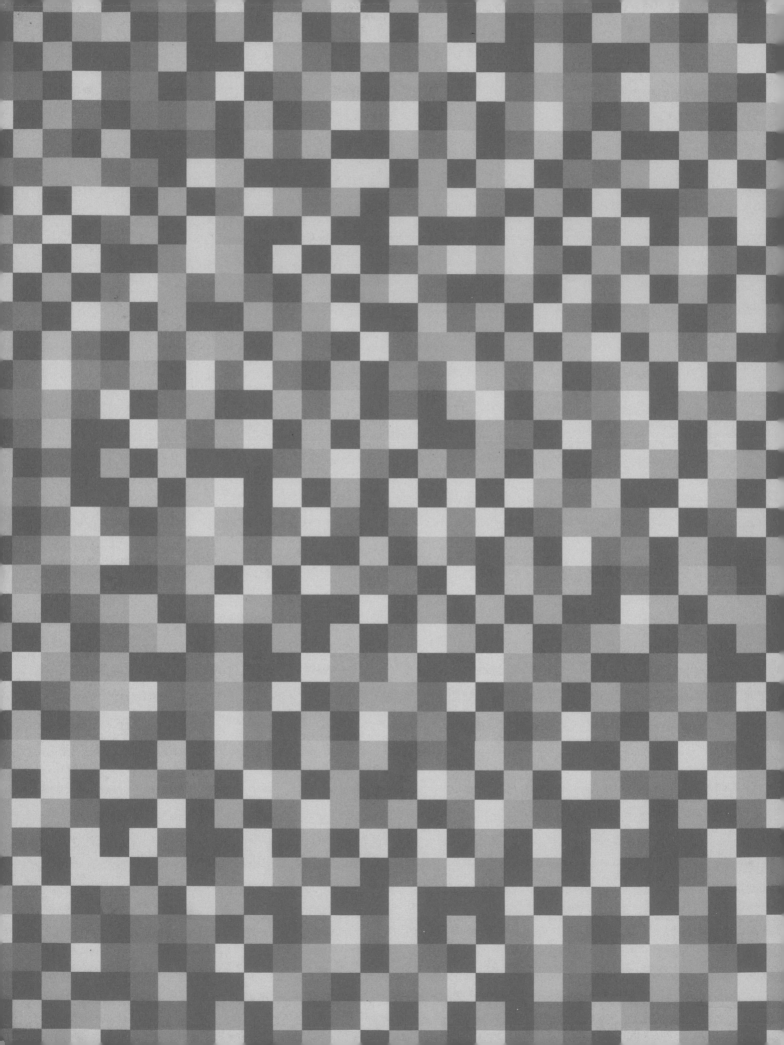